MATERIAL WEALTH
Living with Luxurious Fabrics

MATERIAL WEALTH
Living with Luxurious Fabrics

JACK LENOR LARSEN

ABBEVILLE PRESS · PUBLISHERS · NEW YORK

Editorial Note

Information on the fabrics illustrated, where
available, is given in the caption in the follow-
ing form:
Designer, nationality (where credited)
Fabric name
Fabric composition
Technique/treatment
Dimensions (width, repeat, as appropriate)
Fabric house/manufacturer

pages 2–3 Jean Philippe Lenclos, *Mira-Karma*,
Mira X AG, Switzerland: *pages 4–5* Jim Thompson
Silk Co., Thailand: *pages 6–7* Lenor Friedman,
Triangles and *Presidential*, Coral of Chicago, USA.

Copyright © 1989 Jack Lenor Larsen

This book was designed and produced by
JOHN CALMANN AND KING, LTD.

Designer: Richard Foenander
Typeset by Wyvern Typesetting Ltd., Bristol.

Library of Congress Cataloging-in-Publication Data

Larsen, Jack Lenor
Material wealth: living with luxurious fabrics
by Jack Lenor Larsen
    p. cm.
  Bibliography: p.
  Includes index.
  ISBN 1–55859–007–2
  1. Textile fabrics in interior decoration. I. Title.
NK2115.5.F3L37   1989   89–6683
747′.9—dc20   CIP

First edition

Contents

AN OVERVIEW

Today interior furnishings have a more important role to play than at any other time in history. A century ago, even simple houses were still hand-built, endowed with expressive materials and a distinctive structure; their sites were often personal. Even empty, they presented some character, something to look at, to like, to identify with.

Because of spiraling costs and the dwindling in number of skilled builders, custom building, in most parts of the world, has become rare. It is regrettable that prominent architects only occasionally can afford the vast amounts of time necessary to design individual residences, and that an ever-smaller percentage of would-be home owners can afford to engage them. As a result there are hundreds, even thousands, of distinguished new houses being built, but these represent a decreasing percentage of the total. Most houses and apartments built today are impersonal. Whether stacked up in high-rise blocks or strung along a street, they are too often as alike as peas in a pod. In fact, many people can distinguish home and office from their neighbors' only by the number on the door. Such spaces have neither textural interest, nor a sense of structure, detail, or craftsmanship: in short, they lack architecture. These are shoeboxes of monotonous surfaces — many of them destined for early demise.

When so many aspects of contemporary life are conformist and mass-oriented, it is imperative that the interior spaces be particular to the individuals who live and work in them, fulfilling both their psychological and spiritual needs for rooms that provide a sense of roots, comfort and replenishment. These qualities will, of necessity, derive from the furnishings — the furniture; the fabrics, including those for floors and walls; and the various other objects and accessories that collectively express the tastes and personalities of the inhabitants. The primary function of furnishing fabrics, therefore, is to differentiate and personalize spaces and to give them a sense of place. It is not so much a physical function as a psychological one. These fabrics please the sensibilities as well as the senses, providing privacy, shielding us from glare (or counteracting darkness and gloom), and muffling noise. And at the same time,

Tricia Guild of London shows complete mastery of the potential of printing on textiles, understanding how to transform plain white cotton into splendid amalgams of color and pattern. She also understands the attraction and resurgence in popularity of flowers in pattern — more popular now than in the last fifty years. Her coordinating collections ensure successful combination and selection and probably make her unique among her peers.

Grandiflora Collection
cotton
screenprinting
Designers Guild, UK

of course, they make rooms more physically comfortable, protecting against drafts and making chairs and floors pleasanter to sit and walk on.

Besides giving a room individuality and providing a sense of security and of identity, furnishing fabrics can compensate for the artificial quality of urban life by introducing organic rhythms, shade and shadow, lively surfaces, and contact with natural texture. Mankind was born into a world of fiber: the grasses and trees of the natural environment, the skins we originally wore, even our sinews and tissues are fiber. Because of this, we still have a natural affinity to fabric.

Fabrics may also maximize light, provide privacy, and enhance a view. Their inherent acoustical and insulating properties have never before been so necessary. Because fabric must compensate for the lack of texture, structural expression, detail, proportion, and grace in so many of today's rooms, the emphasis in current interior design is more on the "surround" – that is, the ceilings, walls, and floors – than on furniture and other movable objects. Moreover, of all elements of interior design, fabric offers the greatest range of choice and, hence, the greatest scope for individual expression.

Before we examine fabrics in more detail, we should define some terms. The words "cloth," "fabric," and "textile" are used somewhat loosely by laymen; however, they have quite specific meanings within the field of interior design and related industries.

Cloth is generally understood to include all pliable planes of any fiber or type of construction. Cloths may be woven, knit, knotted, or composed of meshed fibers, such as felt.

Fabric, a broader term, encompasses all kinds of cloth plus rugs and carpets, mattings, basketry, tapestries, and compound structures such as quilts and laminates. Paper is a fabric of meshed cellulostic fibers, leather is a natural fabric of meshed protein fibers.

Textile is a more specific term for fabrics that are woven on a loom. Although most scholars agree with this precise definition of textiles, the textile

departments of museums collect at least all cloths, and, usually, all fabrics — including mats and baskets — as well as embroidery and lace.

Fabric making was the first craft to be industrialized, and remains the largest industry. Although furnishing fabric is a relatively small segment of all fabric produced, the fabric impact of an average room is as likely to be in furnishings as in apparel. The difference is that furnishings are less often hidden in closets, they endure longer, and are less given to the whims of fashion.

The range of different fabrics lumped together under the term "interior fabrics" is enormous. They include those made specifically for use in curtains, draperies, and upholstery; carpeting; bed, bath and table linens; and utilitarian fabrics such as mattress ticking, sheetings, and burlap (hessian). Occasionally apparel fabrics, such as suitings, are appropriated for furnishings.

Types of Fabric

The hundreds of names applied to fabrics over the centuries are derived from all sorts of different qualities and systems of classification. Some, such as "worsted," are named for the yarn from which they are made. Others, such as "satin," refer to the weave; others ("chintz") to the finish; still others ("hopsacking") to the original purpose for which they were used. The relationships are not intrinsic; these names may be parochial or overlapping; they change with time, and may be supplemented or supplanted by trade names devised by yarn or fabric producers.

By describing fabric in terms of fiber, weave, and finish one can achieve such generic yet precise names as "polished silk satin" or "nubby cotton damask." Fabrics are too often designated only by generic fiber type. As the base stuff of fabric, fiber type is important, but not all-important. The grade of fiber may be as crucial. So is the amount of it used (weight), the degree of twist in the yarn-making, the density of weave, and the finish. And, of course, the use: no one fiber does everything best. All yarns have their drawbacks, sometimes grave ones; yet the drawback may itself contribute to the yarn's appeal and be acceptable for certain applications. For example, certain loosely spun wools are subject to wear, and are easily snagged, but their soft, irregular texture may be incorporated to advantage in a drapery fabric.

With fabrics increasingly coded in terms of test results (see pages 225 ff), there is a danger of casting aside some of the finest fabrics, simply because they fail some code or other. Distinguishing fabric by tests or codes is a scientific, not an esthetic, evaluation. But esthetic judgments, too, have their pitfalls where fibers are concerned. They are sometimes influenced by long-standing prejudices — such as, that silk is a prestige fiber, cotton a more common one. But yarns of long-staple Egyptian cotton, combed smooth, then carefully twisted and plied, are far more costly than some spun silks. Another common assumption is that a pure, natural fiber is preferable to a blended one. But purity is not always the supreme virtue. Reinforcing a natural fiber with nylon or polyester may greatly assist its aging qualities.

A wide range of pattern and textural effects is achieved with a minimum variation of color and material in the fabrics shown here, designed by Anne Beetz of Belgium. (For details see pages 152–3.)

The preparation, spinning and plying of fibers affect both their appearance and their physical characteristics. Most natural fibers grow in staple form – that is, as separate, short-to-long fibers. These are normally carded before spinning. They may also be combed, as the long-staple wool fibers used for worsted. The combing removes any short fibers and leaves the rest lying parallel, which accounts for the remarkable smoothness and sheen of the spun yarn and the cloth woven from it.

Of all the natural fibers, silk is the only one produced as a continuous filament. By contrast, all manmade fibers are produced in this form, being extruded through some kind of spinneret analogous to that of the silkworm. These filaments may be combined to form multi-filaments or cut into short lengths for spinning. Multi-filament synthetics may also be bulked in several ways to give them more loft and apparent bulk in relationship to weight.

Attesting to the new vogue for richly patterned furnishings are the jacquard-woven tapestry upholsteries seen on every market. These combine as many as six to eight sets of colored warps with two or more wefts, making many textures and color tonalities possible. Large repeats are also available, with many patterning options.

Esteban Figuerola, Spain
Anatolia
cotton
jacquard tapestry
width: 54½ in. (140 cm)
repeat: 15¼ in. (39 cm)
Esteban Figuerola, SA, Spain

Color and Light

The choice of color in a furnishing fabric should depend, to some extent, on the climate and, in particular, on the quality and amount of light. Too often these factors are underestimated. As a general rule, light, clear colors fare best in the tropics. Those deep, rich shades and warm textures that appear cozy in Oslo are leaden in Miami. And for a designer in London to specify fabrics for sun-drenched Saudi Arabia, as some are now doing, is a risky enterprise.

Another relevant factor is the interior light. Over the last few centuries, lighting has changed considerably, and each change has brought with it corresponding changes in furnishing colors. To modern eyes, the intense palette of many eighteenth-century rooms comes as a shock. Such high-key colors on walls and hangings jar with our image of elegant aristocrats in powdered wigs and delicately embroidered silk. But when lighted only by candles, these hues glow dimly – rich, but not gaudy.

With the introduction of more efficient oil lamps and gaslight in the early nineteenth century, interior color dimmed. Fashionably dark interiors reached a height of popularity in the 1870s, dubbed "the Brown Decade." As the twentieth century dawned, the brilliance of electricity appealed as the beacon of growth and prosperity. If too often the incandescent bulbs masqueraded as candles or were subdued under heavy shades of glass beads or tasseled silk, light within a room increased and colors brightened. When Elsie de Wolfe and Charles Rennie Mackintosh – both design revolutionaries in their very different ways – replaced brown walls with white ones in the early years of this century, the new spirit was widely adopted.

Designers who select and commission textiles for widely varying climates and kinds of light must take all of these factors into consideration. Extremes of light levels, whether it be the shimmering sun in a Mediterranean villa or the restful gloom of a cocktail bar, have the effect of washing out color and pattern. The same situation is found in candle-lit restaurants, where fabrics and carpets with rich patterns may be desirable because they count at low light levels. Such patterns are equally desirable for their ability to conceal stains.

Continuity

While the first craft developed by settled communities was pottery, the first so to be practised by the earlier nomadic cultures — and even older than pottery — was weaving. In all traditional cultures, fabrics have been used to create and shape man's living environment. Even now, the life of the nomadic peoples of Central Asia tells us much about the potential of fabric as portable decoration. Their tents are fabric; so are the rugs, cushions, blankets, mats, and partitions within them. Fabrics not only constitute the dwellings of these people, but reinforce their sense of identity. The patterns of some of these fabrics are richly symbolic, representing aspects of the faith, fortune and genealogy of their owners. Such fabrics are familiar and valued possessions. Paradoxically, they can serve a similar purpose in our modern, technologically advanced society. For people on the move, from one high-powered job and city to another, familiar and valued textiles can also provide continuity of place and character, and a sense of permanence.

Conversely, in today's world, in which most of us live in fewer rooms than we would like to have, fabrics may also serve as instruments of change. Although few people now have the storage space (let alone domestic staff) to make possible a full seasonal change in furnishings, there are still such options as making reversible cushion covers, bedspreads, and other such two-sided pieces. If fabric is required on both sides, each side can easily be different. Such enriching "accessory" fabrics as blankets and small rugs can be added, subtracted, or moved from room to room to create evolving, stimulating living spaces. Windows can be transformed with a different treatment: blinds, instead of draperies, or knotted swags (these are discussed in Section II, Fabric Applications, p. 44). Tables can be covered and uncovered. Summer slip-covers still have a place. They look and feel cool. Such transformations can give everyday surroundings a playful air of the unexpected. On the other hand, they may convey the satisfying quality of ritual. In either case, the message is: "This time in this place is special."

Judy Weinert cuts inexpensive prints, or her clients' own fabrics, into wide strips, then handweaves them into rag rugs. Narrower strips are woven for upholstery, pillows, bedspreads, and wall coverings.

Judy Weinert. USA
Duchess Floral Group
cotton
plain weave
Facets/Textile Designs. USA

Contrasts

The least interesting rooms are "of a piece" — either all old or all new, all costly or all low-budget. Generally speaking, the most engaging interiors balance one such quality with quite another. The richest cloths have more appeal when set off by humbler stuffs, and vice versa. Rooms furnished entirely in one period have, at best, a deadly museum quality; some statement in the present tense is an essential element. A common case in point is a reproduction chair frame covered in a copy of traditional fabric; it looks false and insipid. The same chair frame set off by a vigorous handweave has an offhand chic.

This stylistic contrast can, in some cases, be achieved between the architecture and the furnishings. Crisply modern furnishings set in an old stone mill, or Shaker furniture and Welsh coverlets in a modern setting, for example, can have marvelous impact. More often, however, the options are more limited, and the contrast must be among the furnishings themselves. Even so, there are still many opportunities for contrast. In terms of textiles, such opportunities might take the form of playing conventional cloths against the rich texture of hand-crafted mattings, or old quilts against the machine aesthetic of fabrics created for industrial use (screenings, beltings and felts) or against such workaday fabrics as mattress ticking or canvas.

Dramatic contrasts of color can be exciting; but adventurous combinations require a practised eye if they are to be successful. Far easier to create — and potentially just as lively — are contrasts of texture. Few of us avail ourselves of the magical effects that can be achieved with transparent and translucent fabrics. Picture great sweeps of crisp gauze cascading against light from a window, behind the strong silhouette of a cane-work settee, with both set off by the solidity of a plank floor and a box-like chest. Successfully juxtaposing such forms and textures is, of course, the art of composition — happily, an art form in which all can indulge. Any of us, if we put our minds to it, can achieve unity. It is variety and accent that evade us — especially when a generous budget relieves us of the necessity of using our own ingenuity to mix new with old, or richness with something plain or unexpected.

A room resplendent with late Georgian detailing and furnishings is the setting for a plump, skirted armchair. The original fabric was used in Coco Chanel's 1920s Paris apartment.

Amphora Damask (reintroduced 1987)
cotton, silk
damask
width: 50 in. (127 cm)
repeat: 21 in. (53.3 cm)
Brunschwig and Fils, USA

The Fabric Budget

Those who design and produce luxury goods are often accused of catering to the rich. This is largely a misconception. Most people in the developed world can afford some luxury — not all of the time, but occasionally, in some aspects of life. For many people who need to choose among these aspects, the home has priority.

The price of goods is only one factor in the real or total cost. Quantity is more significant than price per yard or meter: only when large amounts are required does price become a factor. If four cushions or chair seats can be cut from one yard or meter, price is not important. Then, too, fabric cost is only one aspect of a chair or a drapery installation. Take a chair, for instance, that costs 600X and requires $2\frac{1}{4}$ yards (2 meters) of upholstery fabric, plus 75X in delivery charges. If a 20X fabric is used, the total cost is 720X; if an 80X fabric is selected, the total cost is 855X. The chair covered with the more costly fabric is not 300 per cent more expensive, but only about 19 per cent. If the latter will also look good for twice as long, it is the obvious bargain.

Another important consideration is the cost of eventual reupholstering. While applying upholstery in the factory is relatively inexpensive, custom upholstering (plus pick-up and delivery) is not. And because workroom labor charges are rising far faster than the cost of the fabric, the price of reupholstering may equal that of the original purchase. Over a ten-year period the chair covered with the budget fabric (now re-covered) may have cost 1,300X, or about 52 per cent more than if it had been covered with the costly but durable fabric. Although such dramatic contrasts are less likely in the case of draperies or upholstered walls, where the fabric accounts for a greater proportion of the cost, here, too, it is important to think in terms of total installed cost, rather than simply the price of the fabric.

Let us suppose that you have 2,000X to spend on furnishing fabric for a house and a total of 200 yards (or meters) is required. If you restricted your purchases to fabric costing about 10X a yard or meter, the result would be a balanced budget — and some dull rooms, with nothing very special in them.

A brocade inspired by Japanese obis is opulent in the scale and complexity of weaves and colors used. Such a cloth is costly, not only to produce but to prepare for production and to sample.

Kimono Woven Texture
cotton, viscose
continuous weft brocade
width: 54 in. (137 cm)
repeat: 24 in. (61 cm)
Brunschwig and Fils. USA

Moreover, this approach might work to the detriment of much-used seating, on which a relatively durable, usually more costly fabric is required. A bit more money spent on such important fabrics could be balanced by, say, using window shades instead of draperies in one room.

With regard to aesthetic values, the purchase of a small amount of a splendid designer fabric could give much needed character to a room. This might be simply hung on the wall to serve as a focal point or cut up to cover six plump sofa cushions. Or it could be a colorful old rug or quilt. Any of these could be sufficiently decorative to allow a very simple, inexpensive fabric to be used elsewhere in the room.

More than most, Designers Guild collections can claim to be just that – not an assortment of worldly designs introduced at the same time, but a carefully edited selection of printed and woven cloths within a singular theme, palette, and designer's "handwriting." For those decorating with such cloths the assignment is easy: the only mistake would be to let the fabrics be the only statement.

Designers Guild. UK
Spring Flower Collection
cotton
screenprinting
width(s): 160 in. (152.5 cm)
repeat(s): 12¼ in.–31½ in. (31.5 cm–81 cm)
Designers Guild. UK

Chair:
Ravure Moderne
rayon. silk
jacquard damask
Brunschwig and Fils. USA

In the case of dining-room chair seats, only a small amount of fabric will be needed; and here it should be possible to invest in fabric that is not only durable but also decorative, without drastically exceeding the budget.

Here, a word should be said about the difference between "expensive" and "costly." The word "expensive" carries with it a suggestion of imprudence, and even overtones of the related word, "expendable." "Costly," by contrast, suggests value. Today, almost all real estate is costly; so are handmade brogues and fine upholstery leathers; but all of these may be sound investments. So may be the pleasure of a long-remembered, if costly, evening out, or of owning something worth treasuring — for example, a costly fabric. Conversely, the word "inexpensive" can be applied to fabrics that are honest and unassuming — canvas, for instance — whereas "cheap" carries overtones of the shoddy, inadequate, or pretentious.

The New Focus on Design

In fabric production, as elsewhere, the post-war trend has been to simplify and standardize production methods, eliminating distinctive, color-woven cloths in order to build a large, profitable middle market. This trend often meant displacing yarn-dyed cloths in favor of converted ones — that is, weaving literally miles of undyed goods, then making this unfinished cloth particular through such conversion techniques as printing, piece-dying, embroidery, or special finishes. These conversion processes made production easier, faster, and cheaper. Cloth inventories were smaller or more flexible, and delivery time shorter. For the mass market, this approach still has appeal. In terms of style, however, it has serious limitations; it is incapable of producing the sophisticated approaches to weaving shown on the following pages.

An approach parallel to converting plain goods has been the quest to get from fiber to fabric in as few steps as possible. Felts and other non-wovens, made of fibers already colored before extrusion, are ideal in this respect, avoiding both the spinning and weaving processes altogether. Such fabrics roll off production lines as fast as newsprint. Fabric films such as printed or

For a dozen years, the Fabric Workshop in Philadelphia has invited artists, architects, and designers to develop printed fabric in their workshops. The premise is that those new to fabric printing will bring fresh stimuli to the media; they often do.

Shown below, a tablecloth developed by potter Richard DeVore from the dramatic crazing of his tall vessel (Requiem: 7×30×30 in.; 18×76×76 cm). At right, a range of the participants' printed cottons include (at center) Robert Venturi's signature pattern for Knoll International.

embossed vinyl are as thrifty. Needle-punched fabrics – those in which hundreds of needles simultaneously stitch through a fibrous batting – also go a mile-a-minute; tufted fabrics and carpets are almost as fast. These are all technological innovations, interesting because they are new, dynamic, and quickly evolving. For the most part, this production is for the mass market – the largest consumer. Tufted carpets in every fiber and quality now bridge all market levels, comprising at least ninety per cent of world production. Embossed, and – often – printed vinyl wall coverings are found everywhere, especially in corridors, and are used in many institutions and easily-affordable hotels. The Japanese employ this technique in interesting ways, including damask-like plays of horizontal and vertical grooves, which pick up ambient

Foliage or verdure patterns are now second only to florals in popularity. This one, in monochrome, is exceptional in its variety of crisply defined, shaded texture patterns. The design was inspired by Dunand's carved glass panels on the French ocean liner, "Normandie."

La Feuille du Dunand
cotton
screenprinting
width: 54 in (137 cm)
repeat: 54 in. (137 cm)
Clarence House, USA

Fanciful blossoms, veined leaves, and butterflies entwine against an ivory ground.

Odalys
cotton
screenprinting, satin weave
width: 59 in. (137 cm)
repeat: 27 in. (68.6 cm)
Boussac of France

light effectively. Most others are, in one way or another, imitative, with short, easily matched repeats and offensively stolid (and soil-hiding) colorations. As such they aggravate the monotony of the walls they cover. Some exceptions are shown in Section II, "Fabric Applications."

One effect of these relatively new, mass-produced-fabric techniques has been to stimulate the older weaving and printing producers and, particularly, manufacturers of textile production equipment, into faster and more flexible methodology. Interestingly enough, some of these "new" methods are conceptually as old as time, and are not in themselves trite or ugly: spiders, paper wasps, and silk-moth caterpillars all produce beautiful "non-woven" fabrics.

Thirty years ago I predicted that the ultimate development in fabric production for the clothing industry would be to make, in one step, not yardage, but a finished garment, in the manner of seamless nylon stockings, in

Furniture spanning several periods is made complete by traditional upholstery detailing, craftsmanship, and trimmings. Both the furniture and the fabrics are from Brunschwig and Fils.

Banquette:
Tante Rose glazed chintz, adapted from a mid-nineteenth-century document
cotton
screenprinting, glazed
width: 49 in. (124.5 cm)
repeat: 28¾ in. (73 cm), half-drop repeat
Brunschwig and Fils, USA

Chair:
Castle Howard Damask
long staple cotton
damask
width: 54 in. (137 cm)
repeat: 34½ in. (88 cm)
Brunschwig and Fils, USA

Trims:
Lilibet series
rayon
Brunschwig and Fils, USA

which millions of pairs are made alike, then automatically sized over heated forms — without cutting, sewing or waste. Somewhat surprisingly, in view of the revolutionary technological developments in other fields, the seamless garment has not progressed quickly; nor has its counterpart in upholstery, a stretchy, chair-size knit "mitten" which could be pulled on and off for cleaning, color change, or replacement. Quite obviously the design of seating incorporating such a revolutionary change in upholstery covers would be momentous — and high time.

Eighteenth-century furniture was also radically different from that of any previous era. Demands for comfort, intimate conversational areas (as opposed to courtly audience rooms), the importation of mahogany, the development of coil springs, fine steel shaping tools and appropriate upholstery fabrics all contributed to this spectacular revolution. So did market demand:

there existed at the end of the eighteenth century a thousand times as many upholstered chairs as at the beginning. The same multiplication ratio is probably true in the democratic market of today. Unfortunately, methodology has not kept up with the new market demand. Most current furniture production has as many parts, connections and processes as had its eighteenth-century counterpart. To achieve this approximation, costs are as high (compared with mass-produced and widely distributed kitchen appliances), and

Chair (RIGHT):
Tabac, adapted from silk lampas (brocade) in the Musée des Arts Decoratifs, Paris
cotton
screenprinting, chintz finish
width: 61 in. (155 cm)
repeat: 32⅝ in. (83 cm)
Brunschwig and Fils, USA

quality, as compared with earlier hand-made examples, lamentably low.

The 1970s prognosis was that automation would eventually permit new ranges of diversification. That is, it would soon be as easy to provide variety as sameness, and the complex would be as readily available as the simple. This has, to some extent, taken place — not across the board and not from the largest producers, where it was most expected — but in specific areas such as computerized inventory control and production scheduling and automated dye formulation. These innovations have permitted creative manufacturers to achieve both variety and complexity, with sufficient profit to invest in second phase developments. These include fast, shuttle-less looms which have helped enormously in maintaining the predominance of woven fabric — especially those fine-count constructions that seemed in the 1960s destined for extinction.

In the decade following the Second World War, many speciality producers, particularly in Britain and North America, either failed or merged into larger groups. Small Continental weavers or printers, often run by long-established dynasties, captured much of the leadership in the high-quality market. They also introduced a measure of automation (such as fast, flexible looms), new families of dyestuffs and pigments (such as dischargable dye pastes and lacquer print pigments), and sound research and development laboratories. Their automated screenprinting reduced the cost of printing with many colors, and achieved such close alignment as to permit unprecedentedly fine line work and half-tone shading (see pages 86–87).

It is fairly well known that the jacquard pattern-making device, based on a sequence of punched cards, is the antecedent of automation and the computer itself. The fact that automation has in the last few decades removed from jacquard patterning countless hours of tedious hand work is less known. Automation has made the flexibility of the jacquard loom applicable to more types of fabric than ever before. Looms with up to eight weft colors arranged in any order desired, and with long pattern repeats, have revolutionized the

For two decades, Manuel Canovas has drawn flowers in the freshest and most delectable colors. Some are abstracted; others, like these, are more representative of their subject or inspiration.

Manuel Canovas. France
Bien Aimée
cotton. basket-woven
screenprinting. chintzed
width: 55 in. (140 cm)
repeat: $43\frac{1}{2}$ in. (110.5 cm)
Manuel Canovas SA. France

moribund textile industry. The *direct jacquard*, which will go through the steps between a photograph and a floppy disc instructing the loom how to achieve pattern and color, will soon be in common use.

Technological innovations of this kind have made it possible to produce high-quality fabric in appropriate quantities and at low enough cost so that they can be sold at a profit to a market satiated with the standard product. This development has taken place in both fashion and furnishing fabrics; and from 1970 onwards, especially in Italy, Switzerland, Finland, and, later, the area around Lyon, in France, the two have often been produced from the same plant. Time-honored weaving and printing techniques which had for decades been considered too elaborate and expensive to sell in adequate quantities are again flourishing. Warp-printed and discharge-printed fabrics (see pages 73–75), pleated cloths, both woven and converted (see page 151), and tapestry upholstery fabrics, to name just a few, have found their way back into favor. In two decades we have moved from utter simplicity to astounding complexity. This is an unexpected and amazing reversal.

Improvements in fiber and yarn production have kept pace with those in weaving and printing. Long-staple Egyptian and fine Pima cottons are now more abundant, and are generally affordable. Fine worsteds, often polished, flood the office furnishings market, silks abound, luxurious fine linens are returning. And the newest generation of man-made fibers and their blends often look and feel better than their predecessors. Properly selected, the new synthetics fill many requirements, especially those of the larger markets. Earlier shortcomings such as static, pilling, and dirt retention have, in many cases, been resolved.

We should not forget the production of hand-woven fabrics in the developing world. Although these remain a small percentage of even the top end of the market, they have grown in importance, in variety, and in influence. The interaction between American designers and the hand-weavers of Southeast Asia, the British and Japanese working in India, and French teams in

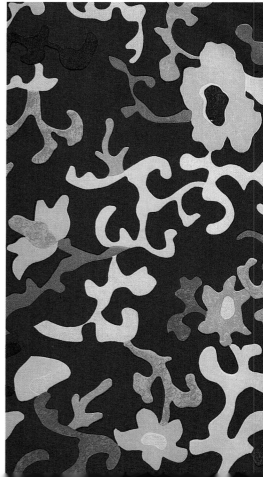

RIGHT
*More recent than his floral prints are Canovas'
blooming damasks. They are energetically
drawn and attractively colored; like many
recent Canovas fabrics they are woven of rayon.*

Manuel Canovas. France
Pamina
rayon, cotton
damask
width: 51 in. (130 cm)
repeat: 43½ in. (110.5 cm)
Manuel Canovas SA. France

LEFT
*This recent Italian print collection (Il Risveglio)
uses flower images at once surreal and
primitive. Appropriately, the colorings are as
idiosyncratic as the patterns, making a naive
and refreshingly direct statement.*

ABOVE
Lynne Wilson. with Centro Design
e Communicazione. Italy
Rerosso
cotton
screenprinting
width: 54½ in. (140 cm)
repeat: 25¼ in. (64 cm)
Assia SpA. Italy

BELOW
Lynne Wilson. with Centro Design
e Communicazione. Italy
Alice
cotton
screenprint
width: 54½ in. (140 cm)
repeat: 25¼ in. (64 cm)
Assia SpA. Italy

China has produced new and remarkable hybrid fabrics drawing on traditions of East and West. Most of these fabrics combine Western design with Asian silks, or South American handspun wools or Indian cottons. In other cases (notably the modern revival of ikat – see page 66) the design employs an ancient technique practised in the home country. These traditional designs, in turn, influence the design of Western fabrics, including those for the mass market.

Most of the batiks seen outside Indonesia are the "forbidden cloths" of central Java, until recently reserved for use by the aristocracy. Conventionally, the traditional symbols of these cloths were soberly colored in indigo, brown, and white. However, both in her book Batik *and in the collections for her American fabric house, China Seas, Inger Elliot favors the florid patterns of Java's north coast, which are influenced by the China trade and, through the Dutch colonials, the coloring of Art Deco.*

RIGHT
Inger Elliot. USA
Palms
cotton
batik-dyed
width: 39–40 in. (99–101.6 cm)
repeat: 37 in. (94 cm)
China Seas. Inc.. USA

LEFT
Inger Elliot. USA
Batavia
cotton
batik-dyed
width: 52 in. (132 cm)
repeat: 25¼ in. (64 cm)
China Seas. Inc.. USA

*An extraordinary painting of festoon cords and
passementerie tassels ornaments a heavy chintz.
Both prints on this page are remarkable for
their drawing and screen engraving, and for the
dozens of colors printed in perfect registration.*

Kazumi Yoshida, Japan
Cafe Royale
cotton
screenprinting
width: 48 in. (122 cm)
repeat: 48 in. (122 cm)
Clarence House, USA

*The border pattern, above, is a reasonably
accurate rendition of Kashmiri embroidery,
while the field evokes a vision of Eden. This was
designed for the twenty-fifth anniversary of
Clarence House by Antonio Ratti of Italy from
his collection of antique Kashmir panels.*

Silver Jubilee
cotton
screenprinting
width: 54 in (137 cm)
panel length: 112½ in.
(281.25 cm)
Clarence House, USA

Although these richly patterned, heavy upholsteries appear similar, their weave constructions are quite different. "Dragon Empress" is a weft brocade; "Vedure" is a "tapestry weave" dependent on several sets of colored warps that admix with several wefts to achieve the many shaded tonalities.

LEFT
Dragon Empress
wool and cotton
weft brocade
width: 54½ in. (140 cm)
repeat: 16½ in. (42.5 cm)
Etro, Italy

BELOW
Vedure
cotton
tapestry weave
width: 59½ in. (151 cm)
repeat: 27½ in. (70 cm)
Scalamandré, USA

"Class Production"

Many people, it seems, are confused as to the descending hierarchy among textiles, from unique, one-off "art pieces" down to mass production. Certainly art students talk as though there were nothing in between. The truth is that there are many gradations of quality in fabrics. In the main, the fabrics in this book are luxury furnishings, and in Britain and North America are available through interior designers and architects. In Europe there are also fine retailers who carry such stuffs, particularly those more contemporary in style. We might call this category "class production."

Mass production at its extreme would have 500 looms in a single shed pounding out blended fiber sheeting, eighteen shifts a week. Class production is quite different. Production runs are small, often of only 250 yards or meters and sometimes less. Successful producers in this market have an open-minded, experienced design team, which is highly regarded by the management of the firm. Their design development is not subordinated to production and marketing, but central to it.

In such firms, timing is crucial, quality control paramount; sound decisions must be made quickly. Often working directly with top designers in fashion or furnishings (sometimes both), these producers are attuned to the cause-and-effect relationships in their particular market. Not infrequently the research and development teams at the mills are as creative as the designers working in the fabric houses that distribute the goods.

In furnishings, the class market is where innovations begin. Too often this is also where they end. Some of these concepts can readily be applied in the larger market. In the case of cotton prints, quality can be comparable, but

Fabric patterns showing decorated Chinese porcelains have recently become popular. This one and Canovas's on page 31 are unusual in that they contain fancifully rendered, colorful peony blossoms.

Osborne and Little
Peony Pots
cotton
screenprinting, glazed

width: 54½ in. (140 cm)
repeat: 25¼ in. (64 cm)
Stead McAlpine, UK

only if the number of colors is not reduced, or the cloth cheapened, or less care given to color matching or finishing. In the case of color-woven fabrics such lowering of standards is even more common. Although in theory it need not be difficult and time-consuming for the large producer to adjust production methods for a new cloth, in practice, concerns for time and money prevail: large industries are by their nature conservative. The continuous production of such classic fabrics as velvets and plushes is much easier for these large firms. The danger here is price competition, often from regions with newer looms or cheaper labor. Thus, there is a real need for these large producers to be able to diversify. Recent moves towards automation should help them to diversify faster. Fortunately, they do not have to match the frantic rate of change that characterizes the fashion fabric trade, with its several collections annually; the producer of furnishing fabrics can take a slightly longer view of stylistic trends.

For two decades, the Swede, Sven Fristedt, has designed correlated collections of fresh prints for the stylish, moderately priced line of Boras. This group, with only one printed color, offers three scales of scattered motifs (left) in fifteen different colorings (right).

Sven Fristedt, Sweden
Noppe, Leva Loppan Collection
cotton
screenprinting
width: 58½ in. (150 cm)
repeat: 27¾ in. (71 cm)
Boras, Sweden

Collections

Interior fabrics of all types, including carpets and linens, are now frequently introduced as a series of rather tightly coordinated collections. The component parts of a collection may have in common a certain type of yarn or weave, color, theme, pattern or intended use. They might include two harmonizing patterns, one large and one small, or perhaps contrast a stripe with texture-patterns and solid colors.

The group may be limited to the several (and growing) number of bed linens required for the well-dressed bed; or it may comprise all the different types of fabric needed to decorate a room. In all cases, the object is to make selection easier for the customer.

From the producer's point of view, being able to use the same yarns, dyestuffs, processes and finishes for several patterns is a welcome rationalization — although these advantages are offset by the need for precise color matching. At best, these collections provide opportunities to create rooms with an aura of custom design — as if all the cloth were made for this installation. The inherent weakness is the potential lack of variety, particularly in construction and texture, which imposes a quality of the expected and the pre-packaged on a room. Still, collections are certain to prevail, if only because this is the most effective way to present designs and to display them.

The same pattern repeated in fabric and wallcoverings creates both a lively and yet serene impression, against which the plain whites, largely the carpet but also the mantel and porcelains, stand out as strong accents. Such dramatic use of positive and negative is most often seen in modern geometric patterns, but softening with a chinoiserie pattern is easier to live with. One presumes that this is a guest room, as it is both too stimulating and too impersonal for everyday use.

Pirouette. from the Chinoiserie Collection
cotton
satin weave. chintzed
width: 54 in (137 cm)
repeat: 27 in (68.6 cm)
wall coverings: paper-backed vinyl
Charles Barone Inc.. USA

Interior designer Sally Serkin co-ordinates fabric collections for J. Robert Scott in the same deft manner with which she plans room schemes. Here, clean, soft pastels are balanced by strong darks and lights, and hard edges of stripes and a check are offset by the softest of floral silks.

FABRIC APPLICATIONS

Windows

PREVIOUS PAGE
Repps are ribbed fabrics formed by warps or wefts so densely packed as to cover yarns running in the other direction. Grosgrain ribbon is an example of a fine, warp repp. These are not rare, but almost always pleasing. The cloth on the preceding pages is unusual in its checkerboard of warp-faced and weft-faced repps and in its two color tones.

Sina Pearson. USA
Sushi
polished worsted
compound repp weave
width: 54 in. (137 cm)
Unika Vaev. USA

The diversity of window types and effects to be seen today is staggering. Some developments, such as tinted and mirrored glass, are architectural; so is the recent trend towards skylights, which provide light without sacrificing privacy. Where privacy is ensured, some people prefer to leave a window uncovered, especially if the nighttime view — a glittering skyline, perhaps, or an illuminated garden — will counteract the usual black void effect and serve as a decorative feature in its own right.

In most cases, however, some form of window covering is essential. Blinds and shutters of various kinds are effective means of regulating light and shade. In Mediterranean countries, people long ago discovered the usefulness of exterior shutters, which block the sun's rays before they can heat up the window glass. Jalousie shutters, venetian blinds and vertical blinds also reduce glare, while casting cool shadows across the room. An ingenious modern version of the venetian blind principle consists of thin, slatted blinds trapped between two layers of glass, which keep the slats clean. Translucent Japanese *shojis* and opaque sliding screens are now frequently found in Western interiors. The floor-to-ceiling window walls of one Oregon house, magnificently sited facing mountains and the afternoon sun, are protected by a combination of the exterior shutter and the sliding screen traditions; at the touch of a button, huge exterior screens of a dark coated fiberglass scrim move across on tracks — as effective as a pair of sunglasses.

Notwithstanding such clever innovations, curtains and draperies remain the most popular covering for windows, with the greatest potential variety of style and the broadest range of cost. Like stage scenery, they can transform a room to suit the season, the occasion, or the time of day. A striking demonstration of this transforming quality of fabrics is provided by the circular dining room of a modern house in Vancouver, with walls almost entirely of glass. At breakfast or lunch, one has the sensation of eating *al fresco* in the garden. In the evening, when the candlelit dinner table is surrounded by heavy, spun-silk draperies, the atmosphere is both intimate and formal.

In the middle decades of this century, it seemed that draped windows (most often with pinch-pleated, floor-to-ceiling panels on traverse rods) were the only option. Recently, however, we have seen many others. Some, with swags and valances, are traditional. Others, such as this knotted solution, soften the hard edge of the window void and give the frame a new importance, while maximizing the light and the view. Though arched Palladian windows are difficult to curtain, this appears an admirable answer. Curtainings spilling onto the floor are also newly popular.

In addition to making rooms seem inviting and softening the edge between solid walls and light or dark voids, curtains and draperies provide varying degrees of sound absorption. This is true even of some sheer curtaining fabrics — known in the trade as casement cloths. When the Larsen Design Studio proposed dense, luxurious casements for the executive floors of the Time Life Building in New York City, it was explained to the client that the additional cost could be subsidized by their budget for acoustical correction. This fabric would be the best acoustical solution.

The most sound-absorbent of the drapery fabrics are thick and spongy, composed of high-loft yarns separated by air spaces — the same principle as in a thermal blanket. By muffling noise within a room, such fabrics also indirectly reduce the noise level: it has been demonstrated that people tend

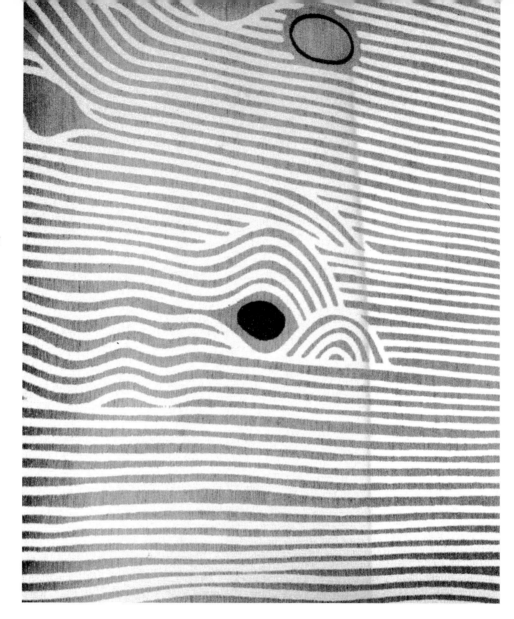

The ground cloth of this fabric was woven with a supplementary warp of cotton; under it is a sheer plain weave of polyester filament. The devoré process burns out the printed cotton areas to achieve a play of translucencies. Small areas printed with an opaque white pigment provide a third level of density.

Gretl and Leo Wollner, Austria
Hydra
polyester and cotton
devoré, screenprinting
width: 63 in. (160 cm)
repeat: 35½ in. (90 cm)
Zimmer and Rohde, Germany; Pontus, USA

LEFT
With a single warp yarn, the organic rhythm of the fabric shown left depends on differential in the "take-up" or shortening rate of those vertical bands that are densely woven and those that are sheer. Pairs of warps are twisted across each other (leno) intermittently, providing dimensional stability. Two very different wefts enhance this quality: one is goat hair, which curls somewhat in the finishing process; the other is a fine gold metallic wrapped around a core yarn.

Jack Lenor Larsen, USA
Jason
Egyptian cotton, goat hair, Lurex gimp
plain weave, leno
width: 52 in. (133 cm)
Jack Lenor Larsen, USA

to lower their voices in quiet rooms. External sounds, such as the din of traffic, are most reduced by heavy fabrics, lined and interlined. Such insulation is also, of course, useful if the room needs to be darkened at times; and it obviously reduces heat loss in winter and heat build-up in summer.

In the case of public buildings, such as institutions and office blocks, building codes often require that window fabrics be tested to pass a specific *shading coefficient* – that is, a numerical rating that measures light transmission in relation to temperature exchange. The lower the numerical rating, the more effective the fabric. The permissible shading coefficient in a given case may depend partly upon the amount and type of glass and the effectiveness of the building's cooling system.

CASEMENT CLOTHS   The 1980s approach to windows is both more sophisticated and more varied than during the immediate postwar period. In those days, when the "picture window" and the glass wall were still relatively new features, few knew quite how to handle them. The tendency was to cover them with a sheer fabric — whether or not they were well proportioned or encumbered with radiators, and whether they faced a private garden or inquisitive neighbors. To be sure, in many cases, this treatment still has merit. At considerably less cost than that of remodeling, one can simply drape the window wall with translucent fabric and so veil the encumbrances or a chaotic view, while giving the room a sense of serenity and modernity. The crucial thing here is to determine which density of fabric is appropriate to a specific room. If controlling glare and providing privacy are both requisites, two fabrics may be needed. An opaque draw drapery over a sheer curtain is the most common solution, but a simple opaque liner under a patterned or printed casement cloth will work as effectively.

The glamorous, translucent fabric, right, is printed with metallic pigment in a special chemical base to elongate fibers and to create the blisters particular to the crêpe plissé process. The large printed areas create a dimension of three inches. The batiklike cracking pattern is planned; so are the shaded color nuances within the lighter areas — a fine example of post-industrial craftsmanship.

Sonesta
cotton
discharge, lacquer printing, crêpe plissé
width: 54 in. (137 cm)
Pausa, Germany

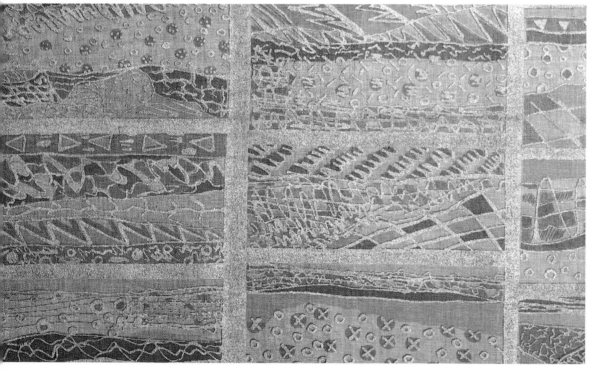

Several pigments, including an outline of reflective silver metallic, produce not only a surface with various responses to light, but, against the light, a pattern with translucent and opaque areas.

Tae Daijima, Japan
Computer
cotton voile
screenprinting (by hand)
width: 54 in. (137 cm)
repeat: 7½ in. (18 cm)
Tae Studio, UK

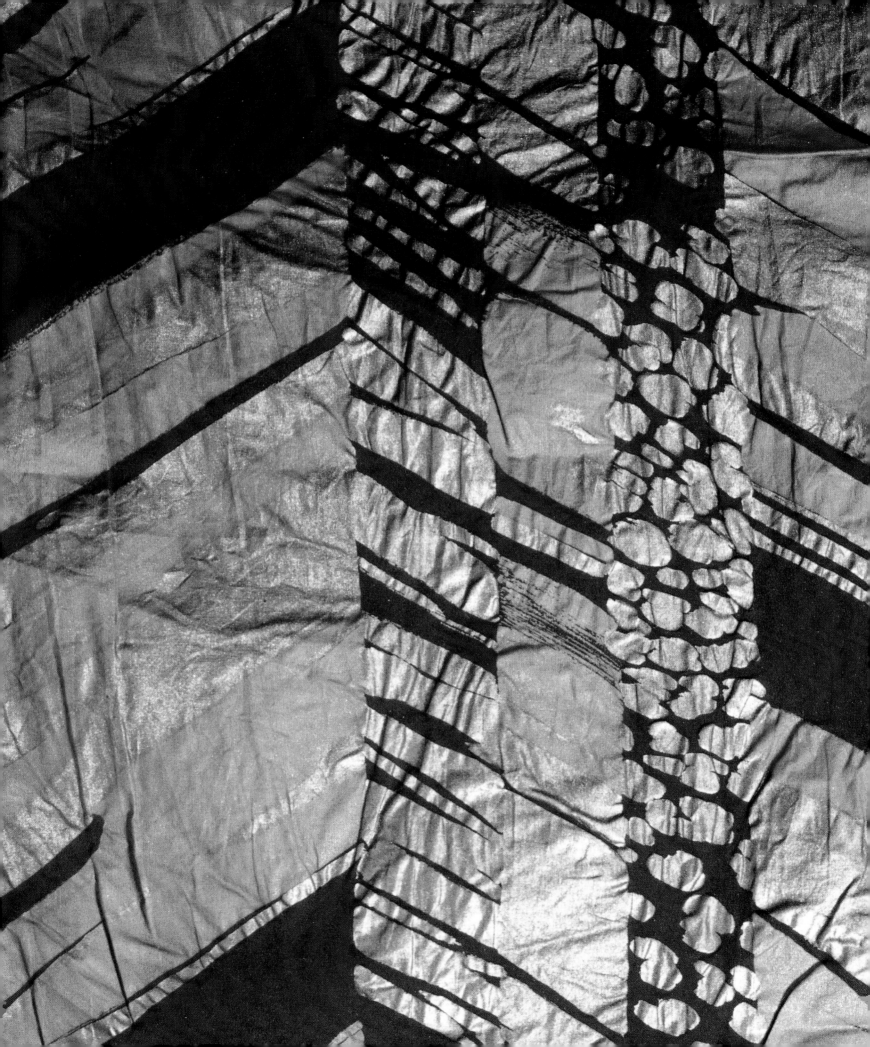

Today's casement cloths are used with discretion – often in tandem with another window treatment, such as blinds, or draperies – and are sufficiently sheer to block glare without excluding light. The selection far exceeds the few wovens and laces of yesteryear; and, at the same time, new manufacturing methods have lowered the price floor considerably. So have the 10-foot (3-meter) widths, hung widthwise to eliminate the cost of seaming. Several man-made fibers which have considerably reduced the risk of degradation in the sunlight can also be heat-set to eliminate shrinking and "yo-yo" – the rising and falling hemline caused by changes in humidity. The more frequent use of tinted glass helps to protect all fibers from the ill effects of heat and light.

Beyond such practical considerations, today's far broader technology has helped to extend the visual range. Printing with silk screens is done quickly and – if the run is sufficiently large – inexpensively, using cylindrical (or rotary) screens, under which the fabric passes automatically. Not only are many colors possible, often with refined half-tone color nuances, but so are a number of seemingly magical processes. Among these are pearlescent and full-gloss lacquers, which are often polished with a steel calender roll after printing, to achieve a patent-leather sheen. Sheer printed voiles are more often given some degree of chintz finish, by being coated with resins and polished with steel rollers in the usual way.

The most popular of these magical processes is *devoré* (from the French, "consumed"), in which a specially woven cloth of sheerest polyester with a supplementary cotton yarn woven in throughout is printed with acid, then heated to such a temperature that the printed cellulostic fiber "burns out" to produce a pattern of two densities. Before printing, the cloth appears to be translucent cotton; usually the transparent layer is polyester, the translucent layer burned out, cotton. Devoré and color printing may be combined, often with an opaque printed pigment to create a third density (see page 49). Because they provide a modicum of privacy and reduce glare without blocking

Coordinating cloths are screenprinted with dye for the color areas and, for the raised outlines, with a chemical flocking liquid which expands after printing.

ABOVE
Gustav Kindermann, Austria
Fantasia
rayon and cotton faille
screenprinting, moiré finish
width: 51 in. (130 cm)
repeat: 25 in. (63 cm)
Atelierdruck Kindermann KG, Austria

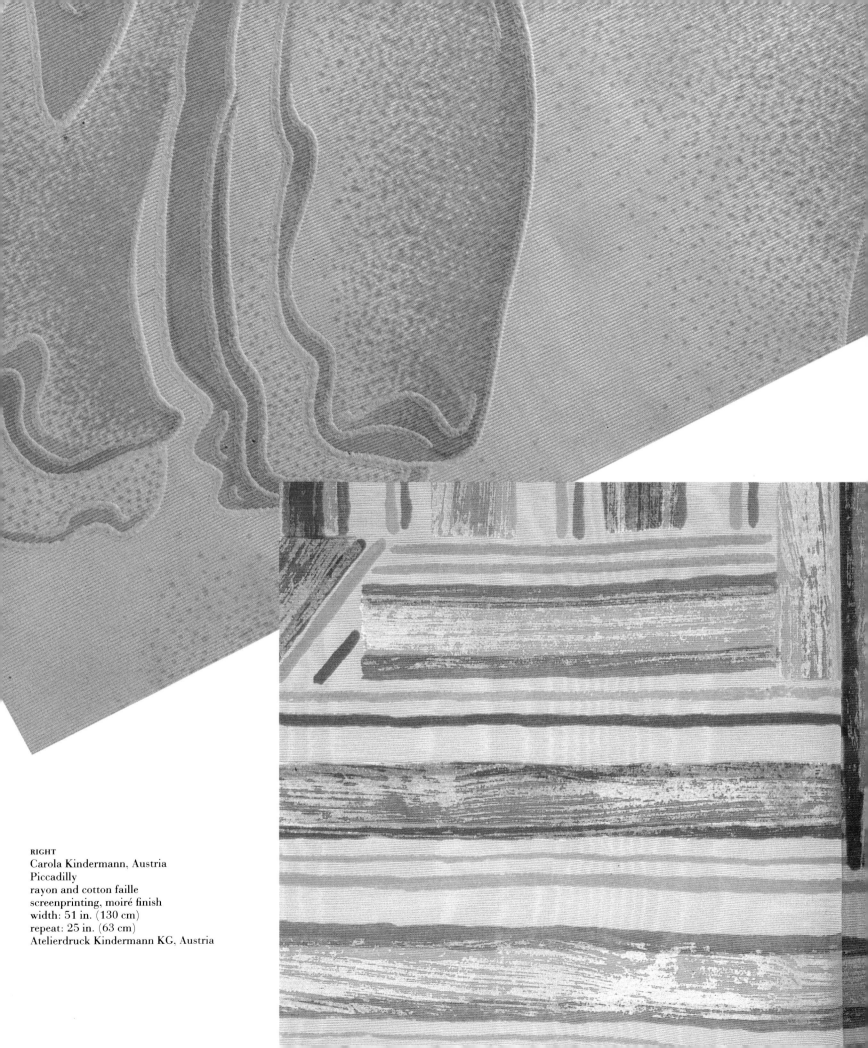

RIGHT
Carola Kindermann, Austria
Piccadilly
rayon and cotton faille
screenprinting, moiré finish
width: 51 in. (130 cm)
repeat: 25 in. (63 cm)
Atelierdruck Kindermann KG, Austria

out precious daylight, devoré curtainings are particularly popular in the relatively gray climes of northern Europe. The two (or three) densities provide a play of light and, depending on the color contrast, may be as subdued or lively as desired.

Crêpe plissé, or printed seersucker (like the one shown on page 51), is not a new fabric; several generations have already worn pajamas of this inexpensive dimpled cloth. What are new are the large patterns and high relief found in translucent, crêpe plissé curtainings. The effect is caused by printing with a chemical agent which elongates fibers so that the printed areas buckle and rise. For drapery weights of fabric, this chemical is often combined with opaque, pearlescent pigments.

Flock prints are made by first applying glue in the chosen pattern, using a silk-screen, and then blowing short, cut fibers over the surface; the fibers stick to the glue-printed areas, producing a characteristic velvety texture. The method is now used less often for fabrics than wallpapers. Glittery Lurex flocked sheers are occasionally seen, however; and there is a new *chemical flock*, which produces raised outlines of expanded foam. Because the foam feels unpleasantly rubbery, the process is perhaps better suited to curtainings than to dual-purpose cloths; that is, those considered appropriate for both draperies and upholstery.

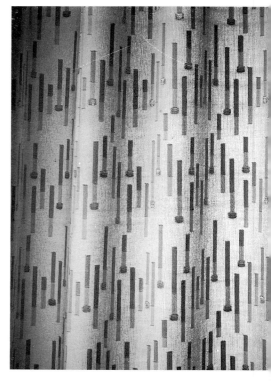

RIGHT
For the translucent grid of this decoupé sheer, three-quarters of the warp yarns have been clipped away. The vertical bars retain either half or all of the warp to achieve different densities. The clipped warp-ends produce a fringelike relief. The base weft, a crépe-spun cotton, lends a pebbled surface. As shown in the lower picture, intermittent gold and silver metallic wefts are also clipped, but on the back of the fabric.

Larsen Design Studio, USA
Posh
cotton, metallic
jacquard warp and weft brocade, clipped
width: 59 in. (150 cm)
Jack Lenor Larsen, USA

FAR RIGHT
This printed curtain is unusual for a combination of processes. First, the cloth was piece-dyed; then it was printed with a chemical in those pattern areas that are now holes. A heavy pigment printed as an outline prevents raveling. After printing, the fabric was heated sufficiently for the chemical to completely burn out the holes. Finally, the cloth was washed and pressed smooth.

Team Création Baumann, Switzerland
Vista
cotton
screenprinting
width: 58½ in. (150 cm)
repeat: 12 in. (31 cm)
Création Baumann, Switzerland

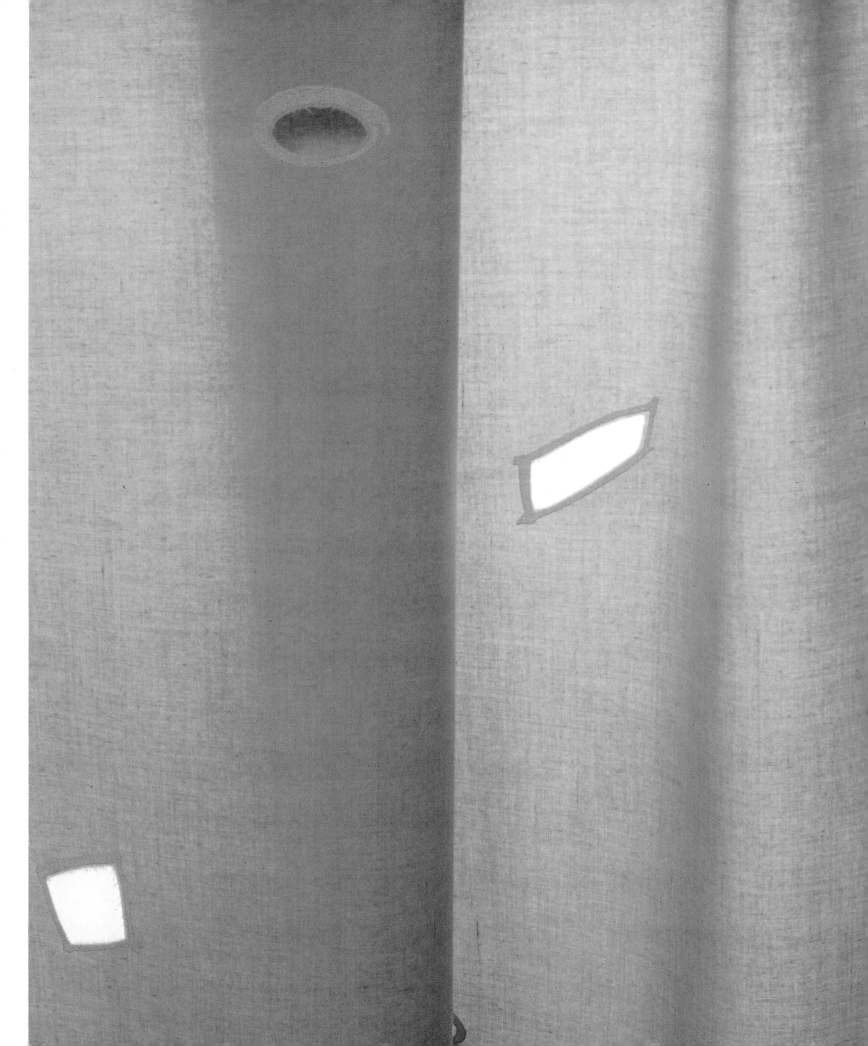

Still another French term, *decoupé* ("cut out"), refers not to a printing technique but to a weaving method in which some threads float over or under the surface in certain areas. After weaving, these are mechanically clipped away, leaving those areas more translucent than the others. Although more costly than devoré, decoupé can achieve far more varied effects and can be used with a greater range of fibers. Some approximate the cut-work sheers of India, which are slowly and less perfectly clipped by hand.

Some *permanently pleated* fabrics are created by washing a layered cloth structure woven with a high-shrink backing yarn. Pleated sheers, however, are invariably a single cloth, which has been pleated in a fabric finishing process. Most are woven of thermoplastic filaments which, when pleated or creased under heat and pressure, are so permanently fixed as to withstand repeated cleaning.

RIGHT
Scattered across an open ground, embroidered moons and stars are alternately opaque or, through cut work, void. Applied rhinestones add a third, light-responsive element.

Heinz Roentgen, Germany
Harem
cotton, polyester, rhinestones
Schiffli embroidery
width: 59 in. (150 cm)
repeat: 47 in. (120 cm)
Nya Nordiska, Germany

FAR RIGHT
Anni Albers, the former Bauhaus weave master and doyenne of twentieth-century weavers, has designed transparent cloths for European production. The most remarkable of these are machine-embroidered on fine cotton voile.

Anni Albers, USA (born Germany)
Monarch (ABOVE). Diadem (BELOW)
cotton
Schiffli embroidery
Sunar Hauserman Europe, Switzerland

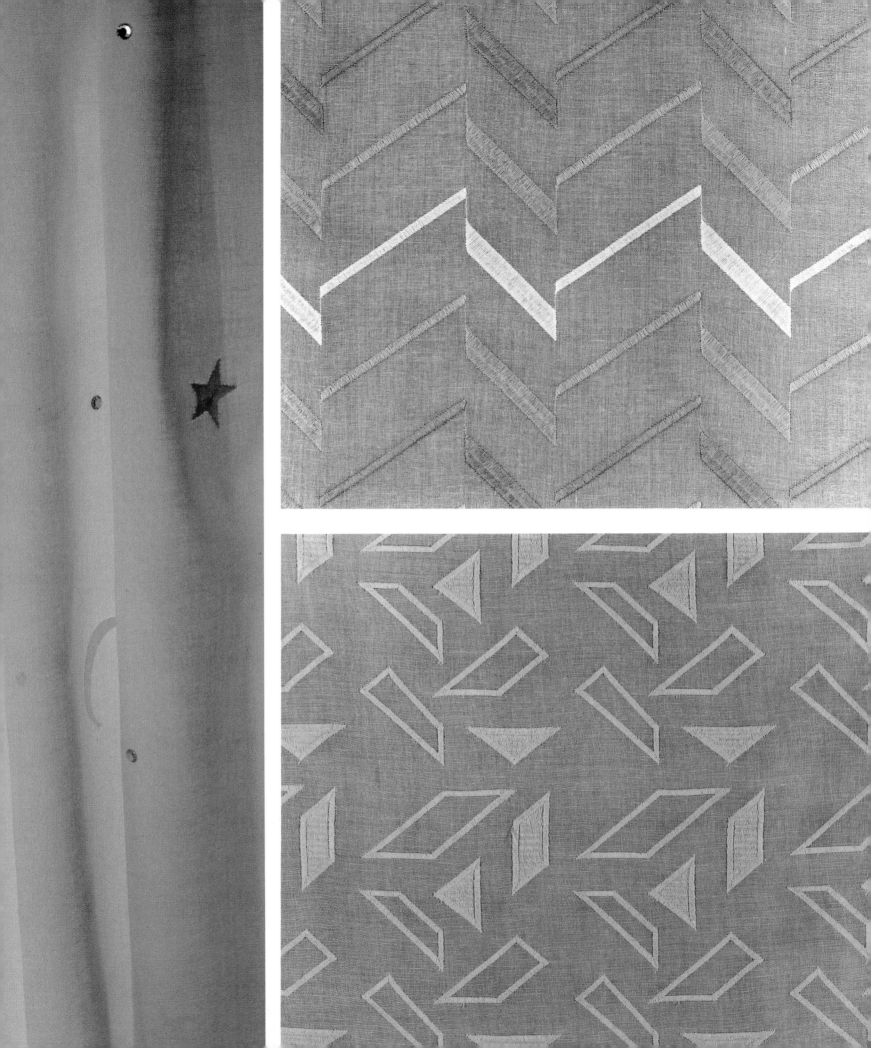

Although these curtainings appear similar, they were made quite differently. The one left is of white poplin, machine stitched to create a hexagonal pleat. The diamond pattern, right, was first printed, then shrunk as part of the cloqué process in which two layers of cloth (doubleweave) are woven to join at set intervals. The high-shrink yarns of the underlayer shorten in washing to achieve a deeply dimpled surface.

LEFT
Team Création Baumann, Switzerland
Pacco
cotton sheeting
machine stitched
width: 56 in. (142 cm)
repeat: 2 in. (5 cm)
Création Baumann, Switzerland

RIGHT
Gianni Versace, Italy
Rilievi
cotton, polyacrylic
screenprinting, double cloth, heat-shrunk to produce cloqué-relief
width: 51 in. (130 cm)
repeat: 1½ in. (4 cm)
Christian Fischbacher, Switzerland

For the sheerest of curtains, fine machine laces have returned to the market in the 1980s. Often these appear as insets and trims; here they are entire panels. Rosalie is a reproduction of a nineteenth-century design.

ABOVE
Rosalie
cotton
Schiffli embroidery
width: 53 in. (134.5 cm)
length: 137 in. (348 cm)
Scalamandré, USA

LEFT
Pamela
cotton
lace, with added detachable border
Brunschwig and Fils, USA

RIGHT
Although Japan's Junichi Arai is best known for his extraordinary apparel fabrics, several of his production cloths lend themselves to furnishings. The opalescent plaid above is entirely woven of finely slit, polarized film.

Junichi Arai, Japan
Check
polyester, titanium-laminated polyester, and nylon films
plain weave
width: 43 in. (110 cm)
repeat: 11¾ in. (30 cm)
NUNO Co. Ltd., Japan

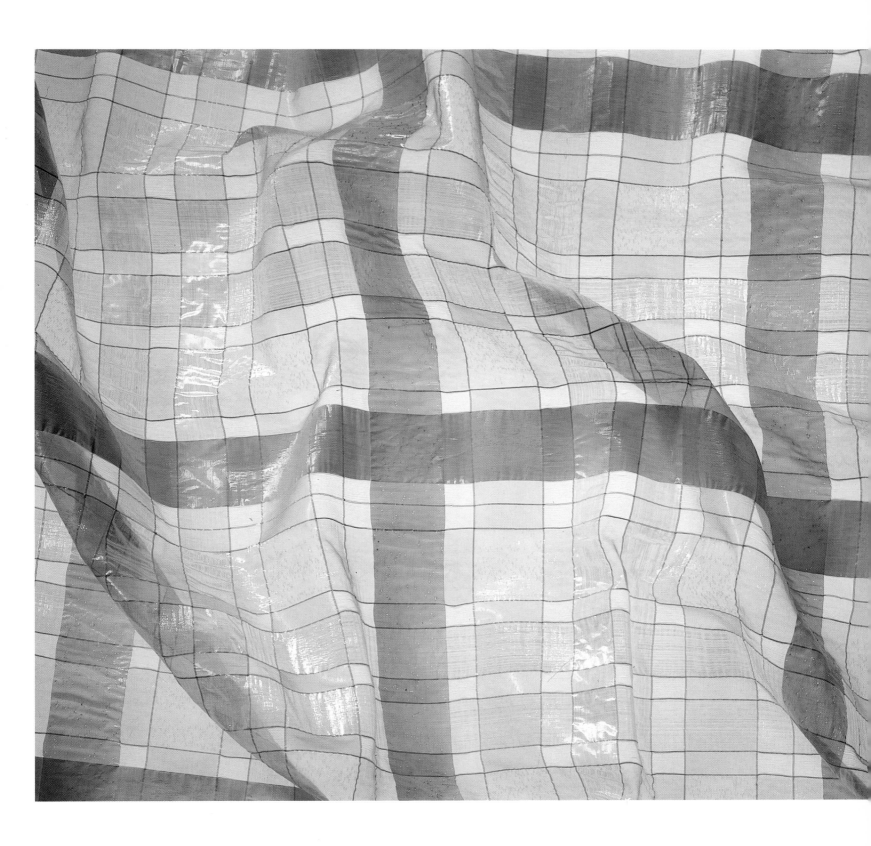

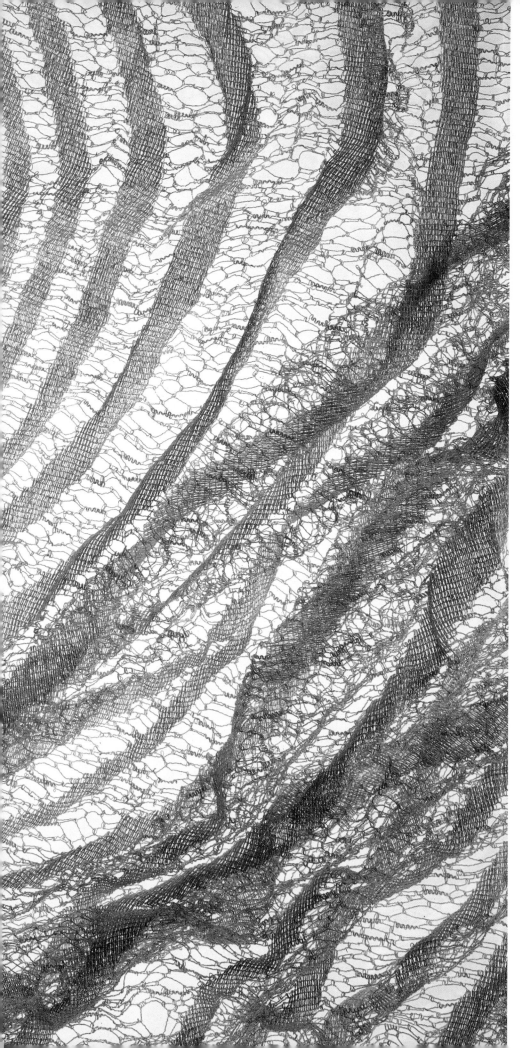

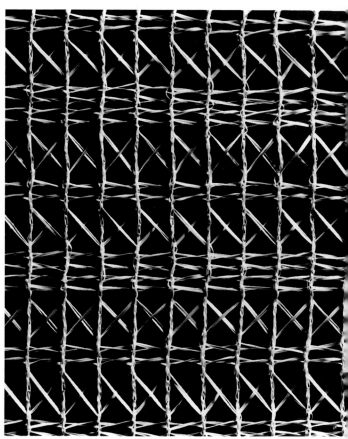

The very large pattern repeat of this knit mesh would be difficult to achieve in weaving. Jacquard knitting on a Rachel machine permits such patterning. The simpler warp knit structure, below, locks in even such slippery yarns as slit films. Heat setting after production makes such knits dimensionally stable.

Junichi Arai and Riko Sudo
Whirlpool
polyester, aluminium-laminated polyester film
jacquard warp knit
width: 93½ in. (240 cm)
repeat: 52½ in. (135 cm)
NUNO Co. Ltd., Japan

Draperies

A certain amount of confusion surrounds the word "draperies." In Britain (and some parts of North America), all fabrics hung over windows are called simply "curtains," and the term "drapery" is confined to fabrics used as canopies of one sort or another. In most of the United States, "draperies" is the term applied to most formal window curtains, from swags and stationary panels to full-width, floor-length draw styles; whereas "curtains" are informal types, including cafe curtains, sheer tie-backs, and full-length glass (in Britain called "net") curtains, gathered onto rods. Ironically, the heaviest and most monumental draperies of all are the "act curtains" of theaters.

Long before they were used on windows, draperies had a variety of other functions, both practical and symbolic. In the ancient world and into the Middle Ages, rich fabrics were draped over thrones to emphasize the pre-eminent position of royalty (and probably, in northern Europe, to protect the royal personage from drafts). The draped bed, which followed, provided privacy as well as warmth as, more often than not, it stood in the great hall.

In the late Renaissance, when houses in northern Europe began to be built with large windows, heavy, lined draperies were hung over these windows by those who could afford to do so. They reduced winter cold and drafts, afforded privacy, and protected fragile, dyed textiles within the rooms. By the eighteenth century, houses, including those of the rising middle class, had become more comfortable. Furniture was commonly upholstered now; dampered fireplaces provided a reasonable amount of heat; and windows were designed and dressed to give greater protection from the weather. Often two layers of curtaining were augmented by shutters and an interlined over-drapery. More efficient heating of the nineteenth century reduced the need for such lavish curtaining, but not the desire for it.

Whereas draperies in the period following the Second World War were often as deeply textured as the client's budget would permit, present-day taste seems to favor smooth and sleek cloths. Lustrous satins, damasks, and repped moirés are often seen. Fibers include silk, long staple cotton, and

Incredible richness has become quite accessible in the last decade through lacquer printing. The printed color is often augmented with fine metallic powders or opalescent crystals reclaimed from the mother-of-pearl in oyster shells. Today these lacquers are usually relatively thin and well bonded to the cloth through pressing under a hot roller.

Isphahan
cotton
lacquer printing
Esteban Figuerola, SA, Spain

worsted wools, occasionally silky mohair from angora goats, and, more often than formerly, fine linen. If simple, inexpensive Nottingham laces are less popular than they once were, fine traditional laces, such as the two shown on page 6, are more often seen. Usually these are used in tandem with a smooth silk or cotton drapery. Fine machine embroidery occasionally decorates sheer curtains or provides a high-luster pattern on drapery fabrics.

      Some of this new richness and diversity is the result of a recent trend among some producers of high-quality fashion fabrics to move into the furnishing fabrics market. Another contributing factor has been the decision

In the 1980s, the silks handwoven in Asia became available in broad ranges of weights, widths, and craft techniques. Two leading producers are Shyam Ahuja in India and the firm of Jim Thompson in Thailand. Ahuja's cloths, left to right, are handpainted taffeta and a warp ikat with a slubby dupioni weft. Ikat refers to yarns tied and dyed to pattern before weaving. Dupioni silk (from the Italian for twins) is produced from two cocoons spun tangentially so that they must be reeled together. The intermittent slubs of the dupioni silk give cloths such as shantung their characteristic texture.

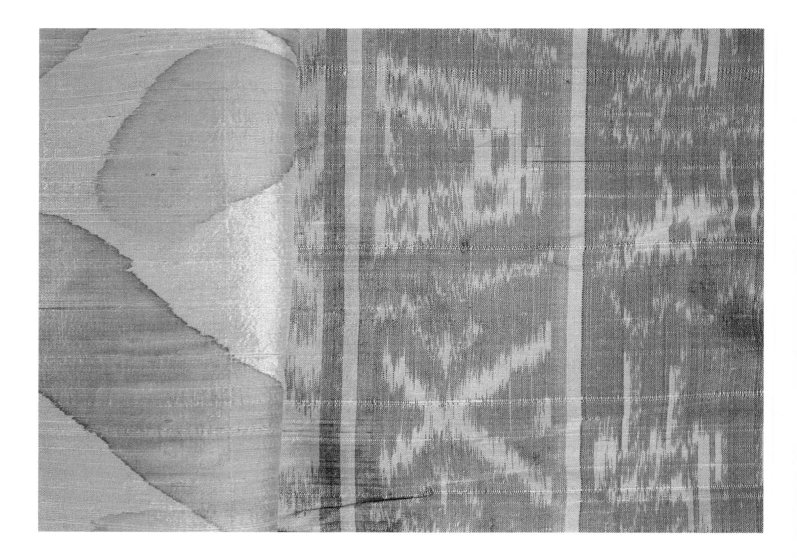

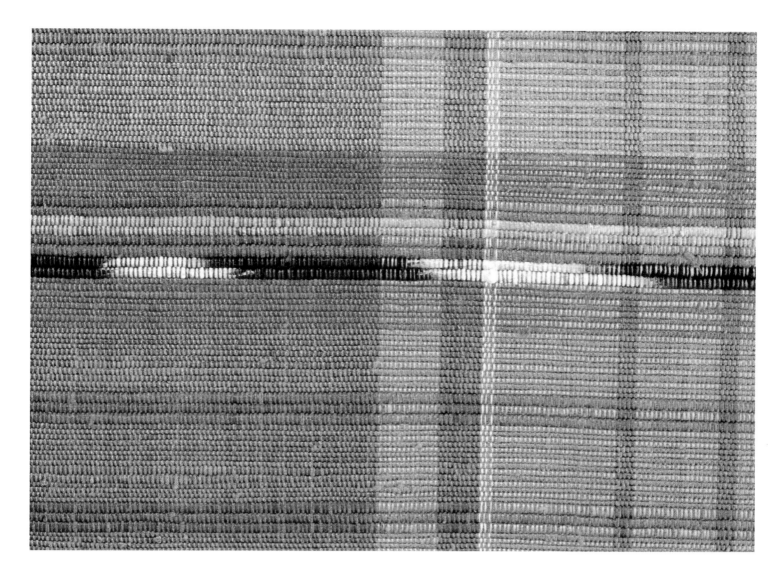

This plaid from Jim Thompson (above) is enlivened with bands of heavier wefts and an accent of weft ikat.

among certain small producers of distinctive, highly individual fabrics to expand their facilities and invest in the considerably faster, often more flexible, modern looms. The entry into the quality furnishings market of such developing nations as Thailand, Korea, China, and India has also enriched the choice of beautiful drapery cloths, particularly silk ones.

Because China — in order to finance industrialization — is annually exporting thousands of tons of silk cloth, yarn, and fiber, silk is more affordable today than ever before. Chinese silk fiber and undyed silk cloth is being woven, dyed, and printed in various countries, notably Switzerland, Italy, India, Thailand, and, to a lesser extent, Britain and the United States. Drapery and wall fabrics are prime markets for this silk and we are the richer for it. The silks most often used for furnishings in earlier decades were textured wild silks, known as tussahs, or cotton-like spun silk (both often incorrectly called "raw silk"); by contrast, the new silk fabrics are of fine, lustrous, reeled silk.

The main difference between wild silks and reeled ones is one of color – the wild silk moths lay eggs in oak trees so the caterpillars feed on oak, and the silk ranges from cream to brown in color. Domesticated silk worms feed on mulberry leaves, and the silk they produce is whiter in color. In addition to this, the cocoons from the wild silk moths are not gathered before the moth emerges, and some fibers will have been eaten through by the moth, so that the fibers of the remaining silk are not continuous but must be spun, at least to some extent. Reeled silk is produced by the domesticated silk worms, and the cocoons are collected intact, producing continuous strands of fiber.

Dupioni silk (deriving from the Italian word for "twins") is produced by two cocoons formed together, the silk from which is reeled together. Because of this there are occasional slubs in the yarn which gives the characteristic texture, considered so desirable that Dupioni cocoons are both sought after and encouraged by silk farmers. All these yarns are well suited to the use of dense poplin and taffeta constructions and the damasks and other jacquard weaves described below.

The use of silk for draperies raises the problem, often voiced by designers, of its susceptibility to deterioration in sunlight. Although it is true that silk fiber tends to be vulnerable to "sun rot," the degree of vulnerability varies according to the type of silk and the construction. The worst cases are those silk cloths with heavy horizontals (wefts) supported by thin or sparse vertical (warp) yarns. Some unlined silk draperies have proved quite durable; nevertheless, a lining is recommended. Since a quality make-up specification calls for a 4- to 6-inch (10- to 15-centimeter) turnback, or side hem, which – directly exposed to sun – will fade and rot long before the face fabric, it is a wise economy to purchase an extra length of cloth, which can be used to replace the turnbacks when this becomes necessary.

The quadrangular figures of this gleaming, polished damask capture light like emerald-cut gemstones. Although the term damask is associated with baroque patterning, it simply means the reversal of warp-face and weft-face pattern areas. Here the field is warp-face satin, the motifs weft-face sateen.

Royalty
polished worsted
jacquard satin damask
width: 54 in. (137 cm)
repeat: 2¾ in. (7 cm)
Ben Rose, USA

RIGHT (ABOVE)
In a lightweight fabric Marjatta Metsovaara achieves several color tonalities and a rounded depth by combining damask weaving with alternating yarn colors.

Marjatta Metsovaara, Finland
Coupage (3256)
Trevira CS
jacquard woven
width: 54 in. (138 cm)
repeat: 18⅜ in. (47 cm)
N.V. Albert Van Havere, Belgium

RIGHT (BELOW)
A dual-purpose damask utilizes a double play of positive/negative elements: first, in the freely drawn plant forms produced by reversing cloth faces; second, in the larger checkerboard of parallel vertical lines.

Anna Severinsson and Inger Högberg, Sweden
Garlic
polyamid, viscose, wool
jacquard damask
width: 58½ in. (150 cm)
repeat: 15¼ in. (39 cm)
Kinnasand, Sweden

OPPOSITE
Damasks are textiles that achieve pattern by reversing the two sides, or faces, of the cloths. The two faces may be different in color, as in the twill of denim, or in light reflection, as in solid color satin damasks. Although not true damasks, the cloths shown opposite achieve a light-responsive pattern in a single color through contrasting areas of low- and high-luster yarns. The jacquard spot motifs reflect light so effectively they appear as voids. The heavier, reversible upholstery cloth, "Spot" (right) also combines damask and double-cloth characteristics.

Team Création Baumann, Switzerland
Alhambra
cotton and polyester
jacquard double-plain weave
width 54½ in. (140 cm)
repeat: 4¾ in. (12.2 cm)
Création Baumann, Switzerland

Team Création Baumann, Switzerland
Spot
cotton
jacquard double-plain weave
width: 58½ in. (150 cm)
Création Baumann, Switzerland

LEFT
The increasingly popular discharge printing is a perceptible process that allows the printed pattern to interact with the weave of the cloth. The large plaid is woven. The floral motif discharged over it removes much of the color to read as light on dark. The unprinted plaid fabric is sold as a coordinate.

Renata Weitz, Germany
Orithia
cotton
discharge screenprinting
width: 55 in. (142 cm)
repeat: 13½ in. (33 cm)
Zimmer and Rohde, Germany; Pontus, USA

BELOW
The large baroque columns shown below are discharge-printed on a black cloth, lending an architectural dimension to a room. If drapery pleats are fitted to the black areas, the columns become rounded. This fabric is from a trompe l'oeil *collection.*

Sue Timney and Graham Fowler, UK
Column TS28
cotton satin
discharge printed
width: 48 in. (122 cm)
repeat: 34 in. (87 cm)
Timney-Fowler Ltd., UK

PATTERN   Another major trend in the furnishing fabrics market is the growing popularity of pattern. The jacquard loom is enjoying a revival; damasks abound, especially those so tightly woven that they can be used for upholstery as well as draperies. The 1980s revival of traditional floral prints, glazed chintzes, paisleys and warp prints shows no sign of abating. The current fashion for richly complex fabrics probably has several causes. One is the almost complete fusion of the formerly separate modern and traditional markets. In the postwar period there was a sharp dichotomy between traditional decorating styles and the revolutionary Modernism, including International Style. In interior design, as in architecture, the prevailing modern design was heavily influenced by a populist ethos, which entailed the use of inexpensive materials and simple technology in furthering its purpose of creating a style accessible to all levels of society. At the other end of the spectrum, tradition was asleep, stuffy, confined to museum rooms. The finest cloth producers on the Continent were still gearing up after years of war. Their lines often seemed out of sync with the new lifestyle, and the colors outmoded.

Slowly, however, the purveyors of traditional furnishings, especially fabrics, awoke to discover that new market opportunities were opening up. The first of these was the contract market – and, in particular, the hospitality industry. Fed by several decades of increasing affluence, especially in the West and in the Arab world, the international catering trade has experienced phenomenal growth. This ever-more-luxurious market dotes on richly patterned, traditional-style fabrics, which also have "residential" applications.

While supplying this expanding and lucrative new market, the tradition-oriented textile mills also began to reap the benefits of the hospitality trade's impact on public taste. These "residential" surroundings were far more influential than any magazine photograph could be; and, like nature imitating art, hotel guests were inspired to give their homes a more luxurious, often traditional aspect.

Of course, many other factors have interacted to create a burgeoning

demand for rich furnishings: in architecture, the Post-Modern quest for ornament and lavish materials has had an enormous influence on interior design; so has the trend towards restoring old buildings and finding new uses for them. The nostalgia for periods considered more secure or more gracious has played a part, along with the cachet of styles considered evocative of "old money."

Because they are more adaptable to an existing furniture style and can be used in so many different ways, fabrics have been at the forefront of the revival of period styles. Damask draperies, for example, are a more accessible and appropriate way of adding a period flavor to a modern room than, say, ornate furniture or paneled walls. And the textile manufacturers have been

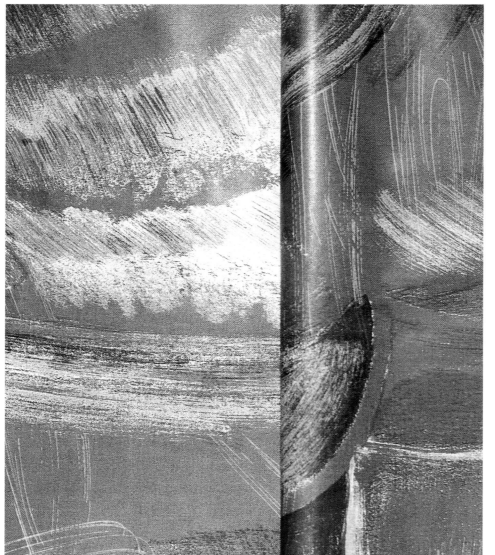

Three new screen prints show effective use of discharge dyes. The silk, above, shows the fine "halo" or light outline between the green printed areas and the ground. Note the contrast between the texture of the color-woven ground and the flat, printed areas.

The surfaces of the two piece-dyed black cottons from Sekers are almost entirely discharge-printed with extremely fine "half-tone" screens achieving subtle blendings with the richness of broken color.

LEFT
Sekers Design Studio, UK
Ikela
cotton
chintzed sheeting
width: 54½ in. (140 cm)
repeat: 36 in. (92 cm)
Sekers Fabrics Ltd., UK

ABOVE
Jim Thompson Design Studio, Thailand
Island Reef
silk
handwoven, discharge screenprinting
width: 48 in. (120 cm)
Jim Thompson Ltd., Thailand

RIGHT
Sekers Design Studio, UK
Istra
cotton
chintzed sheeting
width: 54 in. (140 cm)
repeat: 28 in. (72 cm)
Sekers Fabrics Ltd., UK

quick to respond to each new Retro fashion – from Belle Epoque to Art Deco. Many old established mills have profitably delved into their own archives for their new "best-sellers."

In addition to a new richness in jacquard and print patterning, there is today a wealth of new and old technology. A case in point is the *discharge print* – that is, one made by bleaching the color out of certain areas of a piece-dyed or color-woven cloth, then, often, "inlaying" the bleached areas with another color. By 1970, this process was so seldom used that the dyestuffs required for it were going off the market. A slump in the market for prints brought this process back to spectacular levels and, with it, a sense of craft, of perceptible process. Many discharge prints have a fine "halo" where the color

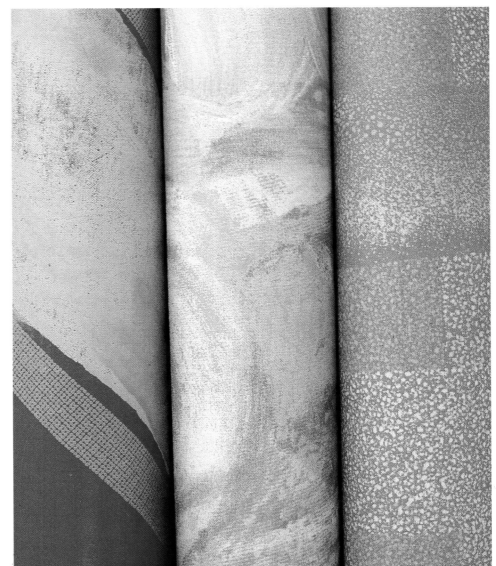

Since the 1970s, fabric embellishment has dominated North American handcrafted fabrics. Under the label of "Surface Design", all manner of techniques are involved, including stitchery, painting, and the ancient resists—batik, ikat, and plangi (or tie-dying)—in such myriad forms as stitch resist (shibori), fold-dyeing, and wrapped resists. Maya Romanoff, one of the earliest to produce plangi fabrics, was also the first to see their potential for interiors. Moving out from Art Environments (three-dimensional structures usually of fabric or other malleable material), he has worked with silk and cotton cloths, canvas carpets, leathers, and, more recently, with wallpapers.

ABOVE
Maya Romanoff. USA/Vandang Srivastava
Pastel Basket
cotton duck
hand-dyed
repeat: 48 in. (125 cm)
wallpaper: Pastel New Stripe
Maya Romanoff Corporation. USA

LEFT
Maya Romanoff. USA
Tiers
Mayachrome leather
resist-dyed, hand painted
Maya Romanoff Corporation. USA

Kyoto Dreams
rayon, fiber, handmade paper
Maya Romanoff Corporation, USA

ABOVE
Maya Romanoff. USA
Shibori
cotton shantung
stitch resist. handpainted
width: 50 in. (127 cm)
Maya Romanoff Corporation. USA

changes. None have a harsh overlay of two printed colors as sometimes happens in direct screen printing.

Particularly from Europe we find prints over damasks and other jacquards. In other cases, warps are printed before weaving – simply, or as damasks or as *double cloths* (patterned fabric composed of two layers, joined where they cross). The revival of *warp printing* (in French, *chiné*) was stimulated by the rediscovery, in the 1970s, of *ikat*, a traditional technique of tying and dying yarns to pattern before they are woven. The distinctive, blurred image that characterizes warp printing evokes the late eighteenth-century prints produced by this technique – themselves inspired by Asian imports.

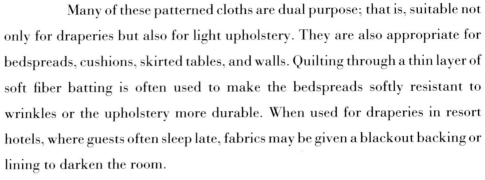

Many of these patterned cloths are dual purpose; that is, suitable not only for draperies but also for light upholstery. They are also appropriate for bedspreads, cushions, skirted tables, and walls. Quilting through a thin layer of soft fiber batting is often used to make the bedspreads softly resistant to wrinkles or the upholstery more durable. When used for draperies in resort hotels, where guests often sleep late, fabrics may be given a blackout backing or lining to darken the room.

Before leaving the subject of pattern, we should note the increasing use of patterned drapery fabrics in furnishings for the health care sector. Pattern, carefully selected and coordinated throughout a space, can enliven bland rooms and give them character. The design of fabrics for this rapidly growing market, which includes nursing and retirement homes as well as hospitals, is still in its infancy.

LEFT
Although most of the new half-tone screens are printed with full coverage, "Mikado" shades only spare bars of full-spectrum color against a white field for a prismatic effect.

Barbara Brenner, Germany
Mikado
cotton
screenprinting, chintz finish
width: 58½/62½ in. (150/160 cm)
repeat: 33⅞/31¼ in. (87/80 cm)
Intair, Germany

RIGHT
The sophistication of the geometry, right, speaks of a stylish Post-Modernism.

Virpi Syrja-Piiroinen, Finland
Poseidon Collection
From right: Zeus, Hefaistos, Appollon
All printed on linen/cotton or cotton satin
width: 58½ in. (150 cm)
repeat(s): 32¾, 31¼ and 34½ in. (84, 80 and 88.5 cm)
Marimekko, Finland

The Helsinki-based firm Marimekko has, since the 1950s, captured an international market with cottons that are printed simply and directly, bold in color, and often overscaled and courageously modern in pattern. Since the death of the founder, Armi Rattia, their new patterns have ranged more widely in style and technique. Still bold, many now use discharge and half-tone printing.

FAR LEFT (ABOVE)
Fujiwo Ishimoto, Japan
Ilma
cotton
screenprinting
width: 58½ in. (150 cm)
repeat: 32¾ in. (84 cm)

FAR LEFT (CENTER)
Satu Montanari, Finland
Hortensia
cotton
satin weave, screenprinting
width: 58½ in. (150 cm)
repeat: 38 in. (97.5 cm)

FAR LEFT (BELOW)
Fujiwo Ishimoto, Japan
Pilvi
cotton
screenprinting
width: 58½ in. (150 cm)
repeat: 117 in. (300 cm)

LEFT
Inka Kivalo, Finland
Vyöhyke
cotton
screenprinting
width: 58½ in. (150 cm)
repeat: 110 in. (281.5 cm)
All: Marimekko, Finland

RIGHT
The Marimekko ground cloths are also more varied than previously. The marble pattern of "Koski" (on the chair) appeals to a wider market.

Chair:
Fujiwo Ishimoto, Japan
Koski
cotton
screenprinting
width: 58½ in. (150 cm)
repeat: 117 in. (300 cm)

Curtain:
Uomo
polyester and cotton
devoré screenprinting
width: 58½ in. (150 cm)
repeat: 68½ in. (175.6 cm)
Both: Marimekko, Finland

LEFT

An abstract pattern is discharge-printed over a black-dyed cloth with a herringbone weave. As the lowest areas of the cloth surface have not fully discharged, the woven pattern is emphasized. Polishing the fabric after printing heightens this effect.

Bernice Christoph-Haefel, Canada
Adrienne
rayon and cotton
discharge screenprinting
width: 54½ in. (140 cm)
repeat: 35½ in. (91 cm)
Zimmer and Rohde, Germany; Pontus, USA

Handpainted fabrics, such as those shown right, have become increasingly popular in the last decade, particularly in France and North America. Part of their popularity consists in shaded effects and a sense of craft not possible in printing. The other asset is their inherent potential for custom patterning and coloring in small quantities. Although figurative patterns are quite possible, rich textures such as these are consistently easier to produce by hand. Shimmering with color, Carolyn Ray's "Semisolid Stripes" recall the translucent quality of onionskin and the metallic sheen of bronze. Created by using two colors laid over each other across the width of the fabric, the result is as neutral as a solid, yet deep with texture.

LEFT (BELOW)
Carolyn Ray, USA
Semi-Solid Stripes
cotton poplin
handpainted
width: 44 in. (111.7 cm)
Carolyn Ray, USA
Copyright © 1985

RIGHT
Ray Wenzel, USA and Mark Feigenbaum, USA
Magic Mountains
silk and cotton
handpainted
width: 50–54 in. (127–137 cm)
Marc/Raymond, USA

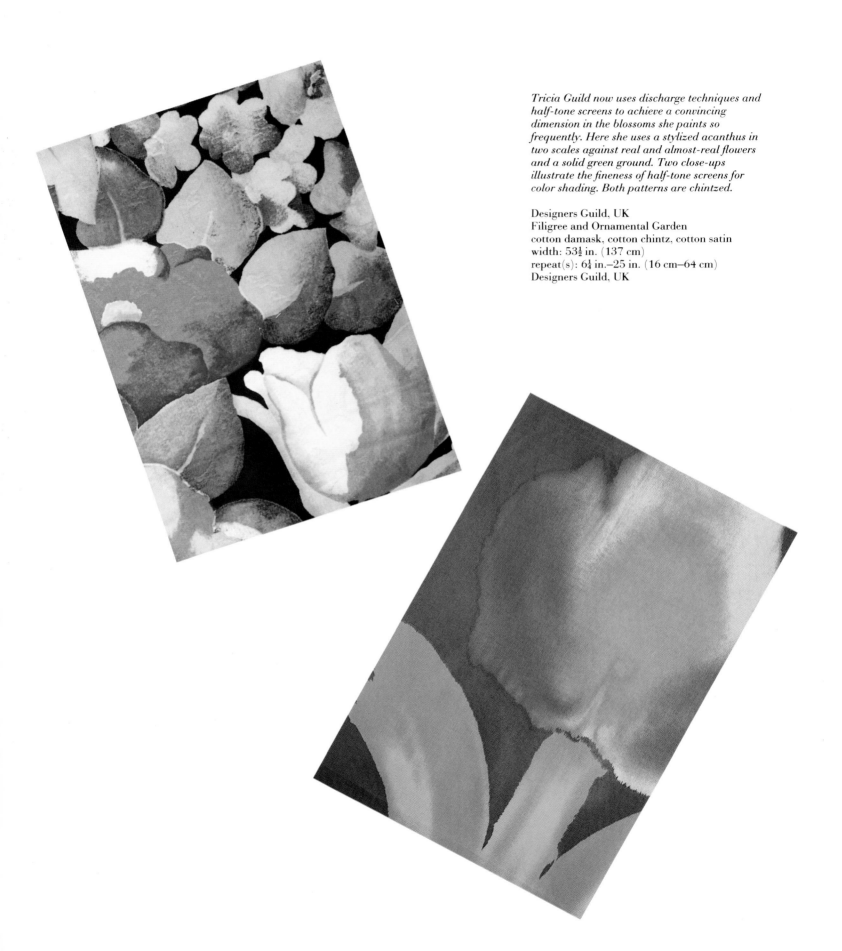

Tricia Guild now uses discharge techniques and half-tone screens to achieve a convincing dimension in the blossoms she paints so frequently. Here she uses a stylized acanthus in two scales against real and almost-real flowers and a solid green ground. Two close-ups illustrate the fineness of half-tone screens for color shading. Both patterns are chintzed.

Designers Guild, UK
Filigree and Ornamental Garden
cotton damask, cotton chintz, cotton satin
width: 53½ in. (137 cm)
repeat(s): 6¼ in.–25 in. (16 cm–64 cm)
Designers Guild, UK

Subtle half-tone shading and many close-valued colors enhance the charm of age and timelessness in two transitional patterns. These suggestions of trompe l'oeil *are fashionable.*

LEFT
Jay Yang, USA (born Taiwan)
Age of Grandeur
cotton
screenprinting, chintz finish
width: 54 in. (138 cm)
repeat: 36 in. (91.5 cm)
Hines and Co., USA

RIGHT
Kazumi Yoshida, Japan
Papiers Japonais
cotton percale (also offered with chintz finish)
screenprinting
width: 50 in. (127 cm)
repeat: 36 in. (91.5 cm)
Clarence House, USA

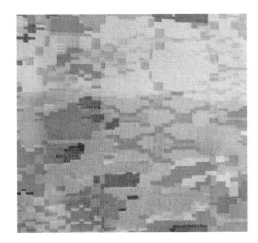

There are many ways to enhance the textural qualities of screenprinted cloths: lacquer printing, discharging, half-tone screens, and patterned grounds. These two use other devices. A simple, wavy-lined "texture screen" printed over both color areas is amazingly effective. An ostrich-skin pattern embossed over a printed velvet provides both a tactile surface and a look of richness and patina.

LEFT (ABOVE)
Bernard Nevill, UK
Phèdre
cotton satin
screenprinting (dye and pigment)
width: 59 in. (150 cm)
repeat: 36 in. (91.5 cm)
Boussac of France

LEFT (CENTER)
Wolfgang Sosnowski, Germany
Tunis
rayon velvet
screenprinting, embossed
width: 54½ in. (140 cm)
repeat: 31¼ in. (v), 53¾ in. (h) (80 cm, 138 cm)
Girmes AG, Germany

Of the many remarkable prints that use neither discharge pastes nor half-tone screens, a great number are revivals of English chintzes and Modernist patterning from the early decades of the twentieth century. The single print color and the clarity of block printing in a discernible small repeat, as seen in the group of reissued patterns above, is typical of "Moderne" prints produced in France between the wars. Still others, such as Capriccio, are Neo-Modern in their patterning, with abstract elements.

OPPOSITE (LEFT TO RIGHT)
Raoul Dufy, France
Les Eccailles, L'Exotique, La Chasse (1928, for Poiret)
cotton duck
screenprinting
width: 59 in. (150 cm)
repeat(s): 7 in. (18.25 cm); 35 in. (91 cm); 30½ in. (80 cm)
Boussac of France

LEFT (BELOW)
Eddie Squires, UK
Capriccio
cotton sheeting
direct printing
width: 52 in. (132 cm)
repeat: 12½ in. (32 cm)
Warner and Sons, Ltd., UK

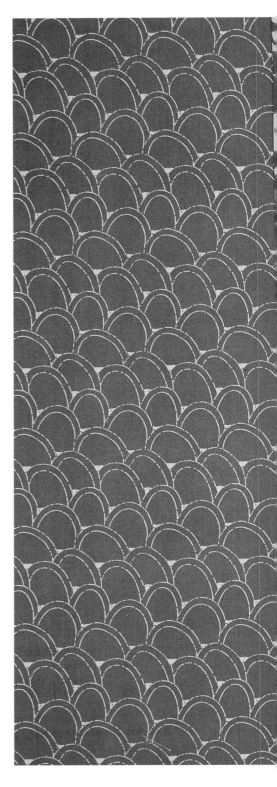

Over the years, Swedish print designers have been those most willing to introduce humor and social elements into their patterning. "Cats," above, is amazingly true to those familiar feline forms and stances. Helen Trast's designs are first painted as watercolors before being adapted to textiles, typified by bright, strong florals and large pattern repeats. Here, she has depicted cockerels, with their tails as whorls over a checkered and dotted ground.

ABOVE
Anna-Lena Emden, Sweden
Cats
cotton sheeting
direct printing, resin treatment
width: 51 in. (130 cm)
repeat: 25 in. (64 cm)
Almedahls, Sweden

RIGHT
Helen Trast, Sweden
Kuckeliku (Cockerels)
cotton sheeting
direct printing
width: 58½ in. (150 cm)
repeat: 45½ in. (117 cm)
Boras, Sweden

After a decade of pursuing "nostalgia" in ice-cream colors, many Swedes have returned to Modernist patterns – often with sharp contrasts of black and white. One manifestation of this return is Kinnasand's Classic Collection, printed by their Ljungbergs subsidiary. When complete, the collection will include patterns by Stig Lindberg, Sven Markelius, and others.

LEFT
Alvar Aalto, Finland
MIT (originally designed for dormitories at the Massachusetts Institute of Technology, late 1940s)
cotton, linen
screenprinting
width: 51 in. (130 cm)
repeat: 1 in. (2.5 cm)
Ljungbergs, Sweden

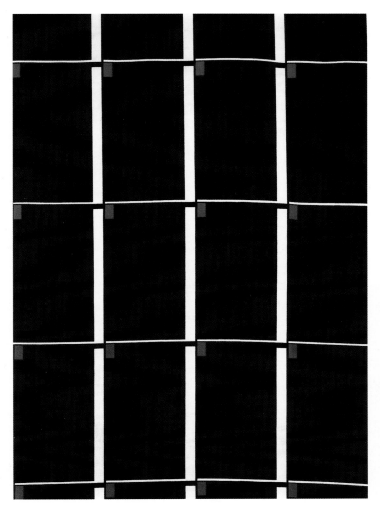

LEFT
Olle Baertling, Sweden
Denise (1954)
cotton, linen
screenprinting
width: 51 in. (130 cm)
repeat: 16¾ in. (43 cm)
Ljungbergs, Sweden

BELOW
Viola Gråsten, Finland
Festivo (1954)
cotton, velvet
screenprinting
width: 51 in. (130 cm)
repeat: 37¾ in. (97 cm)
Ljungbergs, Sweden

LEFT
Karl-Axel Person, Sweden
Delfinsk Rorelse (Dolphin Movements, 1954)
cotton, linen
screenprinting
width: 51 in. (130 cm)
repeat: 45 in. (115 cm)
Ljungbergs, Sweden

BELOW

The axis between designers of Japan and Scandinavia is an old one. It began with reciprocal respect for each culture's handmade tools and containers. When the Japanese looked for prototypes for their postwar furniture industry, the straight lines of Danish teak appealed most. Japan has also adopted the strong, simple format of Swedish and Finnish printed cottons for their multipurpose interior fabrics. Many Japanese graduate students have studied in Finland. A number of them have also designed for such Finnish firms as Marimekko.

Typically diminutive and sparely furnished with small, shaded windows, Japanese rooms seem to call for architectonic patterns and for washable cotton. These are more often selected for futon and cushion covers, table cloths and aprons than for drapery and upholstery.

Shuji Asada, Japan
Oribumitsuzuki
cotton
screenprinting
width: 47 in. (120 cm)
repeat: 5⅛ in (h), 24½ in. (v) (13 cm, 63 cm)
Daiso Co. Ltd., Japan

RIGHT

The grande dame of Swedish design, Astrid Sampe, was for many years director of Nordiska's famous textile studio. There she was responsible for many innovations and a remarkable body of printed and jacquard patterns. Perhaps the most famous of these were the "Signed Textiles" she commissioned with top designers and architects for printing by Erik Ljungbergs in 1954. Some of Sampe's designs are being reissued by Almedahls and Kinnasand. Her "Soft Sand" is printed in black and white, then pleated horizontally.

Astrid Sampe, Sweden
Soft Sand (from the Classic-Contemporary Collection)
cotton muslin
screenprinting, pleating
width: 51 in. (130 cm)
repeat: 16¼ in. (42 cm)
Ljungbergs, Sweden

*The success of Finland's printed cottons grew
out of necessity. After the Second World War,
Finland had some of the largest cotton mills in
Europe, a cadre of talented designers, and no
currency for imports. Printing was the most
expedient route to diversification – and color.
They not only met a need in Finland but
successfully established an export market. For
five decades two styles have run concurrently:
Artek and Voulko have continued with austere
architectonic patterns, while Marimekko,
Metsovaara, Finlayson, and others have led
with a color-rich, organic, and dynamic style.*

RIGHT
Inka Kivalo, Finland
Mosaiikki
cotton satin
screenprinting
Marimekko, Finland

OPPOSITE ABOVE (LEFT)
Artek Design, Finland
Art 4
cotton
screenprinting
width: 58½ in. (150 cm)

OPPOSITE ABOVE (RIGHT)
Alva Aalto, Finland
14/14
cotton
screenprinting
width: 51 in. (130 cm)
repeat: 54½ in. (140 cm)

OPPOSITE BELOW (LEFT)
Sinikka Killinen, Finland
Art 9
cotton
screenprinting
width: 51 in. (130 cm)
repeat: 9 in. (23 cm)

OPPOSITE (BELOW RIGHT)
Elissa Aalto, Finland
H55, Patio
cotton
screenprinting
width(s): 58½ in. (150 cm)
repeat(s): 1⅜ in.; 3½ in. (3.5 cm, 9 cm)
All: Artek, Finland

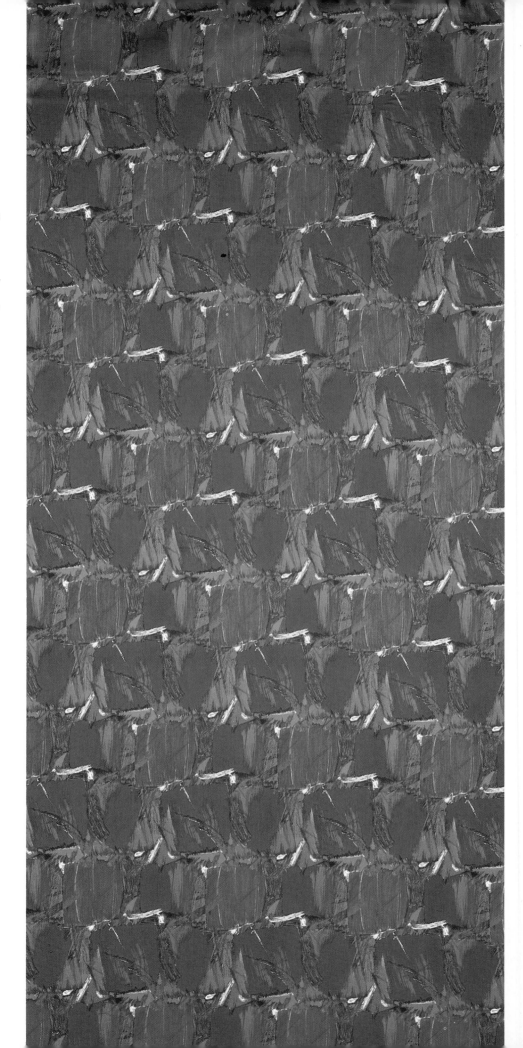

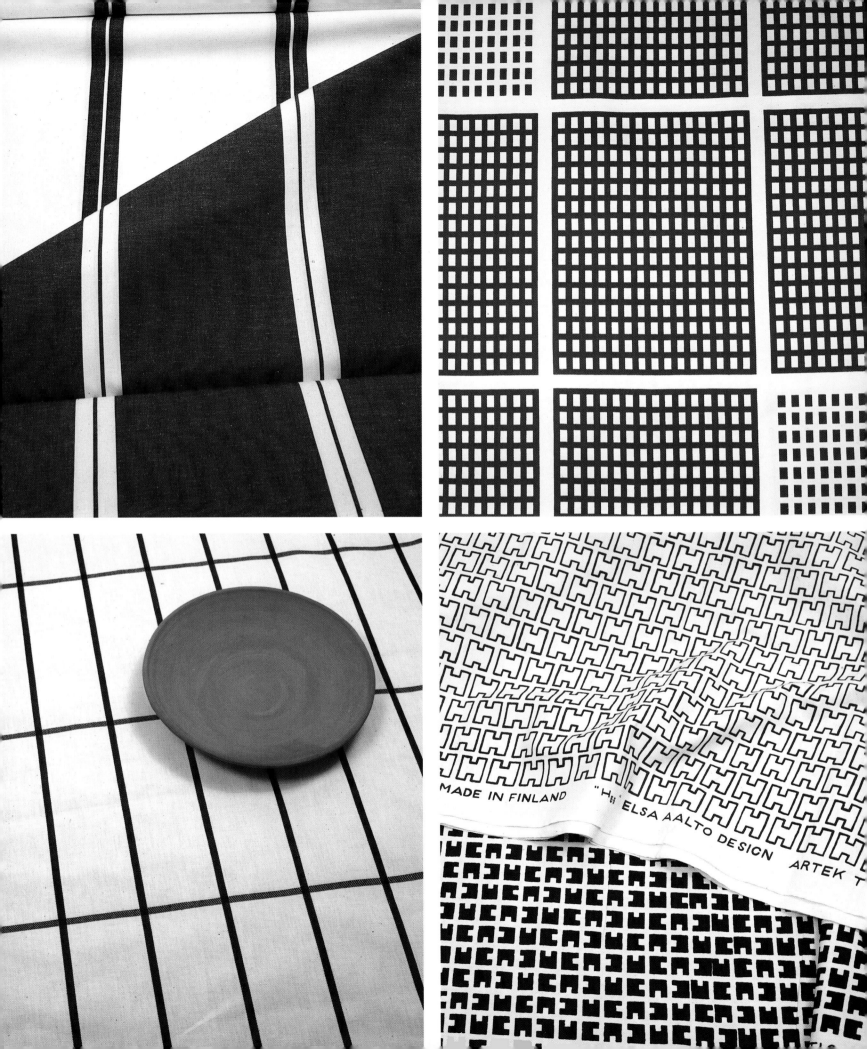

Although best known for woven upholstery fabrics, Denmark has produced a number of internationally recognized print designers, among them Rolf Middleboe, Verner Panton (p. 102) and Bjorn Wünblad. This new design, by Finn Sködt, which faithfully reproduces free brush strokes, is both colorful and playful.

CENTER
Finn Sködt, Denmark
Celeste
cotton sheeting
screenprinting
width: 54½ in. (140 cm)
repeat: 24½ in. (63 cm)
Kvadrat Ltd., Denmark

The printed patterns of Doriano Modeninni are remarkable for their crystal-sharp imagery, related more to painting than the decorative arts.

LEFT
Doriano Modeninni, Italy
Ragtime
cotton
screenprinting
width: 54½ in. (140 cm)
repeat: 39 in. (100 cm)
Assia SpA, Italy

RIGHT
Doriano Modeninni. Italy
Cakewalk
cotton
screenprinting
width: 54½ in. (140 cm)
repeat: 39 in. (100 cm)
Assia SpA. Italy

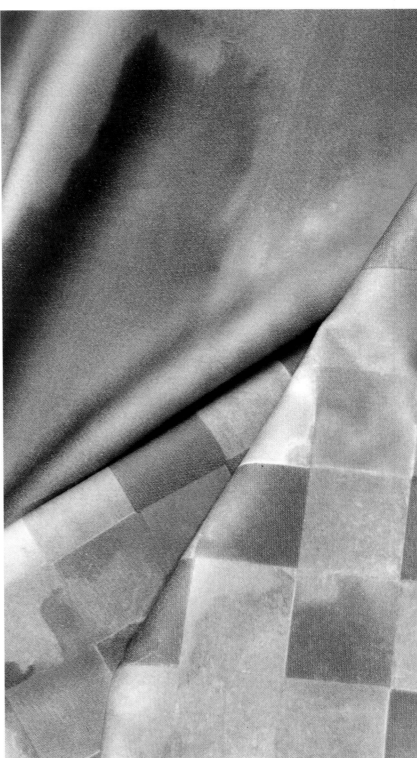

In the mid 1980s the Japanese firm, Fujie Textiles, entered the international market. Because of large production runs, significant technology, and design talent, this outreach has been so successful that we can expect to see more Japanese fabrics, particularly printed ones. These are all from the 1988 collection of designer Hiroshi Awatsuji. Those shown far left and center employ the most subtle of half-tone color effects which are only possible through transfer printing, i.e., the dyes are printed onto a waxed paper, then "transferred" onto cloth through heat and pressure. As transfer prints are most successful on polyester, the cloth here is a polyester-faced satin. The two cloths left are screenprinted on cotton sheeting.

FAR LEFT
Mai
polyester, cotton
transfer printing
width: 53 in. (137 cm)
repeat: 30 in (76.2 cm)

CENTER
Mizu (TOP), Hishi, (BOTTOM)
cotton, polyester
transfer printing
width(s): 53 in. (137 cm)
repeat(s): 30 in. (76.2 cm)

LEFT
Ishi (TOP), Form (BOTTOM)
cotton sheeting
screenprinting, chintzed
width(s): 45 in. (120 cm)
repeat(s): 23 in., 19 in. (60 cm, 49 cm)
All: Fujie Textile Co., Ltd., Japan

A Dane living in Switzerland, Verner Panton
has for many years designed dramatic, colorful
fabrics for Mira X. The latest are lacquer prints.

ABOVE
Mira-Diora
cotton sheeting
screenprinting, pearlized lacquers
width: 51 in. (130 cm)
Mira X AG, Switzerland

RIGHT
Mira-Rubin
cotton sheeting
screenprinting, pearlized and metallic lacquers
width: 54½ in. (140 cm)
repeat: 31¾ in. (82 cm)
Mira X AG, Switzerland

Of all the current developments in printed furnishings, the most dramatic is lacquer printing. First developed in Switzerland, the high-gloss printed areas look as if only they are heavily chintzed, in contrast to the matt-finish ground cloth. Like chintz, lacquer prints depend in part on high-pressure steel rollers both for their gloss and for secure bonding to the cloth. A wide variety of interpretations is shown here and on the following pages.

Three bold strokes in German and Swiss fabric design are discharged and printed on black cloth.

LEFT
Hans Altona, Germany
Oggi
cotton sheeting
lacquer-printed crêpe plissé
width: 58½ in. (150 cm)
Intair, Germany

CENTER
Edi Meyer, Switzerland
Limelight
cotton twill
discharge and lacquer printing
width: 54½ in. (140 cm)
repeat: 17½ in. (45 cm)
Christian Fischbacher, Switzerland

BELOW
Wolfgang Sosnowski, Germany
Venezia
rayon velvet, panné finish
screenprinting, metallic lacquer and pigments (for dulled areas)
width: 52½ in. (135 cm)
repeat: 25¼ in. (v), 13 in. (h) (64 cm, 33.5 cm)
Girmes AG, Germany

OPPOSITE
Janet Taylor, UK
Christmas Roses
handloomed silk, handpainted black paper
screenprinting, metallic lacquer
width: 48 in. (122 cm)
repeat: 48 in. (h), 36 in. (v) (122 cm, 91.5 cm)
Janet Taylor, UK

Like Verner Panton in his recent designs, Jean Philippe Lenclos has also chosen to combine vat dyes and pearlized lacquers with his fabrics Mira-Vonnika (left) and Mira-Karma (pp. 2–3).

LEFT
Jean Philippe Lenclos. France
Mira-Vonnika
cotton satin
screenprinting, pearlized lacquer. chintzed
width: 51 in. (130 cm)
repeat: 13 in. (33.5 cm)
Mira X AG. Switzerland

BELOW
Verner Panton
Mira-Omega
cotton sheeting
screenprinting, pearlized lacquers, vat dyes
width: 54½ in. (140 cm)
repeat: 25¼ in. (64 cm)
Mira X AG. Switzerland

LEFT
Esteban Figuerola. Spain
Los Madras
cotton
screenprinting
width: 54½ in. (140 cm)
Esteban Figuerola SA. Spain

BELOW
Esteban Figuerola. Spain
Los Lacados
cotton
screenprinting
width: 54½ in. (140 cm)
Esteban Figuerola SA. Spain

From Esteban Figuerola, two very different cottons are printed with the same silver metallic lacquer. The free brushwork of India inspired Los Madras, which was first printed with dyes. The stripes and check of Los Lacados are heavily printed over a color-woven iridescent duck. The old Japanese box is handpainted lacquer.

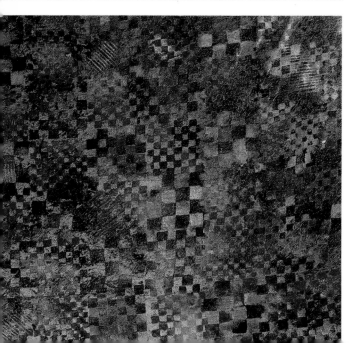

With their strong Byzantine and Middle-Eastern references, the richly patterned panné velvets by Nora and Helen Feruzzi of Norelene seem to exude the atmosphere of medieval Venice. The mosaiclike patterning, reminiscent of St Mark's Cathedral in Venice, is the direct result of printing with a limited number of wood blocks. The impact of beating down the pigment-laden blocks adds a low relief to the cloth. Almost always blocked on silk or cotton velvet, Norelene fabrics are made to order. Those shown here use both techniques and images more freely than the "mosaics," yet the richness of their hallmark craftsmanship is as evident.

LEFT (ABOVE)
Piramide
velvet
block printing
width: 54½ in. (140 cm)
length: 78 in. (200 cm)

LEFT (CENTER)
Punta di diamanti
velvet
block printing
width: 78 in. (200 cm)
length: 86 in. (220 cm)
All: Norelene. Italy

LEFT (BELOW)
Mosaico
velvet
block printing
width: 54½ in. (140 cm)
length: 78 in. (200 cm)

RIGHT
Banchette
cotton
block printing
width: 27¼ in. (70 cm)
length: 27¼ in. (70 cm)

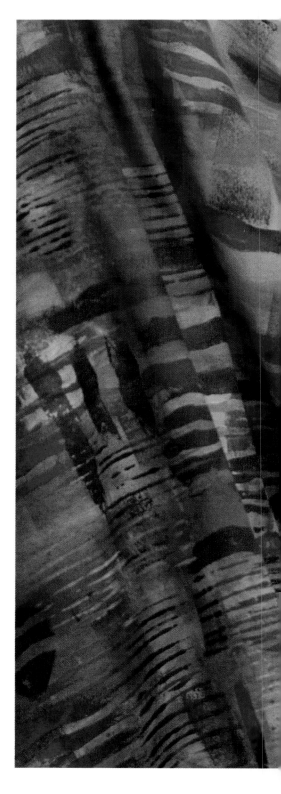

Window Treatments

In addition to the renewed use of traditional valances, swags, and other effects, there is a new fashion for voluminous cloth window shades and shirred fabric blinds, such as Austrian shades and balloon (festoon) blinds, especially for public spaces. Some of these can be stock treatments offered to both professionals and the public by large workrooms at something close to factory prices. But because most consume extravagant amounts of cloth, they can be extremely costly. Those that are custom-made, by skilled labor under exacting supervision, are a luxury, for workroom costs have risen much more sharply than the cost of the goods, and probably will continue to do so.

At the other end of the price scale are those window treatments

The treatment right is similar to the one on p. 46, showing another pleasing arrangement of knotted drapery. (A Westgate fabric.)

While the draperies left do not close, the randomly-pleated balloon shade will raise and lower. Rings at the bottom hem are attached to a series of vertical cords, much like the stage curtains of opera houses. The cascading fabric has an aura of glamour; the treatment is particularly appropriate for windows that do not come down to floor level.

which are not draped but used flat. Usually these require less than half as much fabric as draperies — even less, if only the glass is covered. Because fabrication and maintenance costs are also reduced considerably, a premium-priced fabric becomes quite affordable. Another advantage of a flat window treatment is that it admits relatively more light than any draped fabric, while still screening a view or cutting glare.

One of the best systems of sliding panels of flat fabric is Paneltrac, a prizewinning design available internationally from the Kirsch Company. The panels snap on (and off) carrier strips with Velcro and are weighted at the bottom with aluminum slats. With Paneltrac, drapery pleats can also be created with only the Velcro adhesion, so that workroom labor and cleaning are made simpler. Another increasingly popular "slider" is a Western version of the Japanese *shoji*, using fabric in place of mulberry paper. Designer Patricia Keller, of Hong Kong, uses such sliding panels extensively for resort hotel bedrooms, with fabrics so opaque as to block out all light.

For certain installations, window fabric stretched flat on Paneltrac has several advantages. Here, both the unpleasant near view and the old window mullions are masked; the distant skyline is revealed, and light is maximized, as shown in the single layer, left. As both the fabric used and the workroom labor are minimal, a luxurious, handwoven wool casement could be afforded.

Larsen Design Studio, USA
Accord
wool
plain weave with discontinuous weft brocade
width: 50 in. (127 cm)
repeat: 24 in.×25 in. (61 cm×63.5 cm)
Jack Lenor Larsen, USA

At the other end of the price spectrum, the industrially produced screening, left, is designed to reduce the buildup of glare and heat. To meet differing orientations, a choice of several densities and color values is offered.

Thermoscreen
PVC coated fiberglass
twill weave, heat-set
3G Mermet Corporation, USA

In his Connecticut home, architect Warren Platner uses window seats and window blinds to great effect. The flat roller shade gives privacy and eliminates glare while admitting a softer light. The perfectly centered painted image provides an alternative view.

Other flat window treatments include a host of different shades and blinds. The selection of pleated shades, ready-made, complete with hardware, is now wider than ever and, at its best, both handsome and inexpensive. The newest are woven plastic screenings in an assortment of densities and color values appropriate for various exposures. Roll mechanisms have been improved; some are electronically controlled, even synchronized to rise to the same level. For the Philip Morris Headquarters Building in New York, the Larsen Studio designed four different densities of screening. These look alike from the exterior, but are positioned to give maximum shade at the top of the south façade and progressively less to other areas, down to the bottom of the north façade.

Reasonably enough, climate remains a major factor in choosing window treatments. In warm climates, such as the Mediterranean and the tropics, excluding light and heat remains a key objective. Conversely, fussy, space-filling, warming window treatments are not in favor in these countries. In regions with long winters or normally cloudy skies, it is crucial to maximize light and ameliorate the long, cold nights. In such conditions, a treatment that gives a room a psychological, as well as a physical, sense of warmth – through rich colors, textures, or patterns is obviously to be preferred.

The windows of highrise blocks present a new challenge. Those apartments high above the windows of neighbors can indulge in the new luxury of minimal screening. Almost all such elevated windows, however, are subject at some time of the day or year, to extreme glare, and often create a "greenhouse effect," with considerable heat gain. Because the privacy and the view are dearly paid for, finding a window treatment that both preserves these advantages and minimizes the hazards and extra expense of higher air-conditioning costs and the replacement of faded textiles becomes a matter of critical importance.

The new generation of pleated blinds are ready-made in many widths, inexpensive, and widely distributed. Their permanently stiffened cloths include complex weaves, satin stripes, prints, metalized surfaces, and often minute perforations.

LEFT
Janet Birch. USA
Aurora
polyester
twill woven. metalized for insulation purposes. pigmented finish of interior face; flame retardant
width: 60 in. (152 cm)
Graber Industries. USA

RIGHT
Janet Birch. USA
Dobby Stripe
polyester
satin damask. resin finished. heatset. pleated
width: 60 in. (152 cm)
repeat: $\frac{3}{4}$ in. (1.8 cm)
Graber Industries. USA

Upholstery

Quite apart from those prints and wovens which can serve for drapery or light upholstery is an enormous range designed almost exclusively for furniture. Their requisites are dimensional stability and resistance to both abrasion and soiling. Long floats which could result in snagging are avoided. These fabrics are often too firm for draping and the practice of applying an acrylic backing to reduce fraying and slippage renders them even less pliable. Of course, the search for durability is ameliorated by concerns for appearance, tactile appeal (known in the trade as "hand"), and cost.

Because upholstery fabric is a chief contributor to the aesthetic of many types of rooms, covers must be selected with care. Success, of course, depends on the relationship of the fabric to intended use, to the frame it covers, and to other patterns, colors, and textures in the room. The best balance of unity and variety between covers usually depends on types of frames, other visual elements within the room, and the room's character and size. Here it is difficult to generalize because any rule or guideline can be successfully broken,

RIGHT
The rounded curves of a lounge chair are highlighted by the luster of a polished cotton damask. The rich color patterning is created through a combination of warp printing and jacquard weaving.

Jean Philippe Lenclos, France
Mira-Lorissa
Egyptian cotton
warp printed jacquard damask
width: 55 in. (139.7 cm)
repeat: 28 in. (71.1 cm)
Mira X AG, Switzerland

LEFT
For a small New York apartment Ben Baldwin designed these chairs to be comfortable both for dining and conversation. In order not to clutter the space with too many pieces he augmented them with folding chairs. That the extremely costly tiger-patterned handwoven silk velvet (currently over $1000 a yard wholesale), is used on only one chair makes it both more special and more affordable. The Corbusier painting, right, is hinged to cover a television screen.

Tiger velvet
silk
handwoven jacquard velvet
width: 27 in. (68.5 cm)
Brunschwig and Fils, USA

LEFT (ABOVE)
Upholstery texture may be achieved through a yarn or combination of yarns, by the weave, or by both factors. Concentrating on yarn alone, much in the spirit of the 1940s, Docey Lewis handweaves a soft stripe of mohair bouclé, velvety chenille, and metallic gimp.

Docey Lewis. USA
Makati Chenille
mohair wool. rayon. Lurex. nylon
plain weave
width: 50 in. (127 cm)
Silk Dynasty. Inc.. USA

LEFT (CENTER)
A smooth, hard, undulating rib, similar to the automobile upholsteries of the 1950s, achieves texture through the weave and the alternation of dark and light warp yarns.

Linda Thompson. USA
Christine
cotton. rayon. polyacrylic
weft brocade
width: 54 in. (140 cm)
Sunar Hauserman. USA

LEFT (BELOW)
An undulating herringbone pattern in long repeat gives a sensuous chenille cloth scale and a sense of structure. The smooth, braille-like relief is a pleasure to handle.

Bessan Cotton Chenille
cotton
warp brocade
width: 51 in. (130 cm)
Brunschwig and Fils, USA

RIGHT
While many of the old luxury wools have given way to the fleeces of sheep cross-bred to produce both fiber and meat, superior, wool-producing flocks still exist, often in remote areas. The farmers' cooperative, Manos de Uruguay, produces silky, long-fiber wool, then handspins yarns that are as light and soft as silk, with remarkable mutations of broken color caused by the dyeing of ungraded fiber "in the fleece," that is, before spinning. Much of this yarn is knit into sweaters, but some is kept for handweaving at the cooperative. The results are upholstery fabrics with bold scale and lively dynamics but still sufficiently soft for the bare arms of ladies in evening dresses.

Larsen Design Studio. USA
Luxor
wool
twill weave
width: 50 in. (127 cm)
Jack Lenor Larsen. USA

Small-scale tapestry upholsteries are particularly popular for smaller chairs. Their crisp patterns are soil-hiding. The coordinated coloring here is a direct consequence of being woven on the same (or common) warp. The Archive Collection includes patterns originally drawn between 1903 and 1906 in Vienna.

From left: Hans Vollmer. City (1905)
Josef Hoffmann. Tiroli (1904)
and Paradis (1908)
cotton, viscose, polyester
jacquard tapestry
width(s): 51 in. (130 cm)
repeat(s): $2\frac{3}{8}$ in., $4\frac{1}{4}$ in., $1\frac{5}{8}$ in.
(6 cm, 11 cm, 4 cm)
Unika Vaev, USA

The M. C. Escher Collection is based on original designs by Escher.

Hazel Siegel, USA
Medieval, Graphic, Cygnus
cotton, viscose
jacquard tapestry
width(s): 52 in. (133 cm)
repeat(s): 13 in., $3\frac{1}{2}$ in., $3\frac{1}{4}$ in.
(33.5 cm, 9 cm, 8.2 cm)
Design Tex Fabrics Inc., USA

but, for instance, a chair with fine detailing and, perhaps, a channel back may come off best in a relatively plain fabric. Similarly, a room rich in architectural detail or patterned walls may be well served by a solid color cloth. A variety of seating styles in one room may be unified by covering all of them in one fabric.

Like clothing, upholstery fabric modifies all it covers. One fabric can make a pretty chair look even prettier; another will make it look old before its time. The upholstery will affect the "period" and style of a piece as well as its apparent size and importance. Some furniture shapes are so basic as to accept a wide variety of covers; others will require a thin cloth or a bulky one. Within such categories, however, there are many choices. A "thin" cloth might be a woven silk or a pliable calfskin, plain or patterned, matte or lustrous, and, of course, in any color. The fabric chosen will determine whether a chair is appropriate for boudoir or boardroom, or something in between.

An imaginative choice of fabric can make antique and traditional frames look younger or less formal, or basic, simple furniture more elegant or deluxe. Similarly, contemporary furniture, which tends to evoke offices or hotel lobbies (not surprisingly, as it is often designed with such applications in mind), can be given a softer, more residential appearance by being upholstered in a more distinctive fabric, such as a print or jacquard. Typical reproductions of antique chair frames are more pleasing when the upholstery is not itself a reproduction but a less expected choice, perhaps more rustic or modern, so as to relate to present day lifestyle.

Some fabrics, of course, are so distinctive in style as to be appropriate for only a narrow range of furniture types. Others are so universal as to "work" in any environment. As furniture production becomes increasingly automated, the choice of frames is being reduced, with fewer specific or particular models being offered. This situation, along with the rising price of fine antiques, means that individuality in furniture depends, more than ever, on the upholstery fabric. Fortunately, the variety of fabrics available is rapidly increasing.

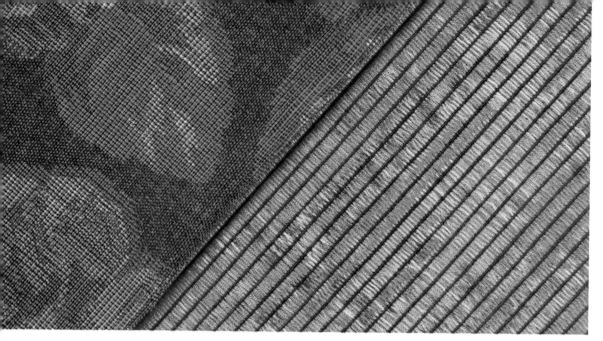

In addition to all the tapestry types woven before World War II, in the 1980s several innovations have appeared on the market. One of the most popular methods is to combine tapestry weave with a cotton chenille weft to achieve a contrast of hard and velvety patterned areas. The opposite is to combine areas of tightly woven "tapestry" with warps floating over a number of wefts in the manner of a ribbed and lustrous ottoman weave. Although the contrast in texture is dramatic, resistance to wear – never high in these cloths – is still further reduced. The fabric right combines both weaves in a single cloth. The fabric shown left uses the same warp for companion fabrics. Still another variation is the combination with cotton of high-luster manmade warp yarns to create textural contrast. As those of rayon have a reduced abrasion resistance, such synthetic filaments as polyester and nylon are being used more frequently, often in tandem with cotton.

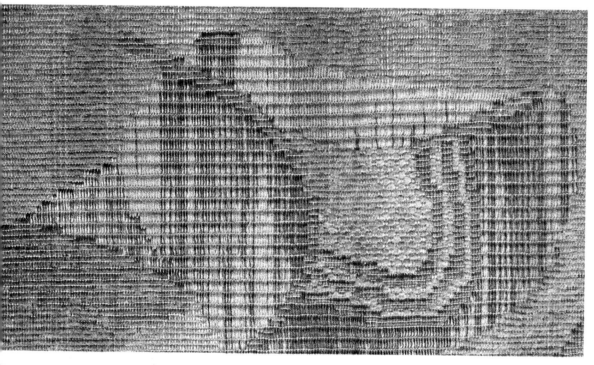

LEFT (ABOVE)
Baku
rayon. cotton
jacquard tapestry
width: 54½ in. (140 cm)
repeat: 26½ in. (68 cm)
de Angelis, Italy

LEFT (CENTER)
Kiev
rayon. cotton
warp brocade
width: 54½ in. (140 cm)
repeat: 12½ in. (32 cm)
de Angelis. Italy

LEFT (BELOW)
The close-up detail left more clearly shows the manner in which these jacquard tapestries are woven. As many as eight sets of colored warps, plus two or more heavier wefts, are mixed to create any number of shades, with potential for deep shadows.

Valdessa
cotton chenille, nylon, cotton
jacquard tapestry
Reidlinger Moebelstoffweberei. Germany

RIGHT
Scalamandré has recently introduced this collection of tapestry borders to make possible architecturally defined wall paneling, window fabric finishes such as valances, tie-backs, and so on. The weave is exceptionally fine and the color shading meticulous.

Gobelin Border Collection
cotton
jacquard tapestry
widths: range from ¾ in. (1.9 cm) to 11 in. (27.9 cm)
Scalamandré, USA

APPROPRIATE CHOICES   In choosing a patterned upholstery fabric, one must respect the shape of the furniture; in particular, its relatively flat planes. Spiraling or diagonal movement, appropriate for dresses or drapery, is inappropriate here. Horizontal and/or vertical patterns suitable for a rectangular sofa present technical and aesthetic problems if applied to a more sculptured chair frame. Because patterns with an implied depth or perspective are visually illogical on a solid object, they should be avoided.

The scale or apparent size of a pattern affects both the piece of furniture itself and the space it occupies. A large bed or sofa, for example, can be made to appear smaller and more compatible with other pieces in a room if it is covered in a pattern which breaks large surfaces into smaller areas. Scale of pattern has as much to do with degree of contrast as with the size of the motifs. The scale of the cloth structure is also important: delicate chairs covered in heavy fabric may appear bloated or bundled; large pieces in thin fabrics may have an air of being undressed.

Seating in which the frame is exposed deserves special consideration, especially in the relationship between the color and texture of frame and fabric. Often the quietest, most unified combination is achieved if the color values of both are fairly well matched. For example, a natural ash frame may look better covered with a pale upholstery than with a dark one. Notable exceptions are such classic frames as Hepplewhite, which were designed for the

Similar to jacquard tapestry in its elaborate patterning potential and in the admixture of colors of several sets of warp yarns is the jacquard frieze (epinglé). Though the look may be somewhat similar from a distance, there are several differences. For one, the durability tends to be far higher because the carpetlike loop-pile surface is similar to thousands of minute springs, which are so resistent to wear that they are the most durable of all upholstery structures (the cut piles of velvet, velour, and plush are almost as strong). The frieze is different, too, in that only the warp yarn is visible, and such quality fibers as worsted and line linen are often used, sometimes in combination with cotton. Prices may be high, but in terms of life expectancy these cloths are costly, not expensive.

ABOVE
Piccolo punto
worsted wool
jacquard frieze
width: 54½ in. (140 cm)
repeat: 13½ in. (35 cm)
Etro. Italy

RIGHT
Persia Epinglé
cotton
jacquard frieze
width: 54½ in. (140 cm)
Etro. Italy

high contrast of light cloth against dark wood. Furniture with exposed frames often requires proportionately less fabric, and if only the seat is covered, it may be possible to indulge in a more costly fabric, both luxurious and durable. Its pattern may be soil-hiding, and because there is little contact with hands, cleaning is less of a problem.

An appropriate upholstery fabric pleases the hand, the eye, and the intelligence. Appropriateness is not solely an aesthetic matter; it entails practical considerations, too. People should not be intimidated by fabrics so pale or delicate as to discourage normal use. If light colors are desired, washable slipcovers may be necessary. Another option is to choose a pattern that will disguise staining. But where use is light, or cleaning arrangements of a high standard, the choice of a light-colored, even delicate, fabric may be appropriate. Such a fabric can have a sybaritic quality more normally associated with evening dress.

As durable as the warp pile friezes just shown is
a post-Second World War innovation in woven
cloth. Invented with pipecleaner diagrams by
Dr Bayani when interned in Austria during the
war, the patterning wefts do not cross the fabric
width but travel only about $\frac{1}{6}$ of an inch
(0.4 cm), then return for the succeeding row in
the manner of true Gobelin tapestry. Combined
with a jacquard, this permits amazing freedom
of pattern; it also allows the weft to be packed
down much more firmly than other weaving to
result in an extremely durable and soil-resistant
surface.

LEFT
Larsen Design Studio, USA
Solarus
worsted wool, cotton
unique weaving process
width: 50 in. (127 cm)
repeat: 12½ in. (h), 17¾ in. (v) (31.7 cm, 45 cm)
Jack Lenor Larsen, USA

RIGHT (ABOVE)
"Illusions," shown with several coordinating
cloths, is a double-wefted jacquard damask
woven as a horizontal stripe but designed to be
"railroaded," i.e., the stripes used vertically
when upholstered.

Boris Kroll Design Studios, USA
Illusions
wool, nylon
jacquard satin damask
width: 54 in. (137 cm)
repeat: 12⅝ in. (h), 6¼ in. (v) (30.6 cm,
15.8 cm)
Boris Kroll Fabrics Inc., USA

RIGHT (BELOW)
In quite a different price range from the pattern
fabrics just shown, is a group of special interest.
The all-cotton jacquards combine the qualities
of double weave and warp-face repp. Because
both the yarn spinning and weaving are
unusually firm, these cloths have – for cotton –
good resistance to abrasion.

Ross Litell, USA
Grafic
cotton, polyester
double cloth
width: 52–54 in. (133–137 cm)
repeat: 2 in. (5 cm)
Rudd Textiles, USA

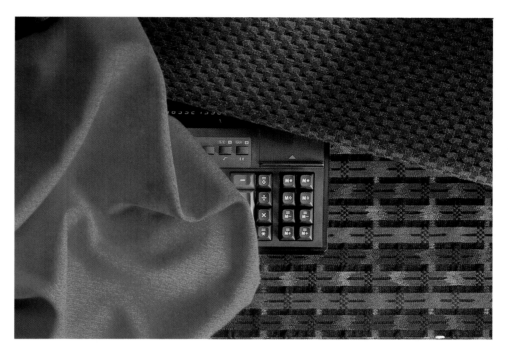

As designer and mill owner, Marjatta Metsovaara van Havere has the freedom to select the mill yarns, colors, and looms, and the responsibility to keep the looms running profitably. To do this she explores the broadest range of weaves, many of them for jacquard looms. As shown, her collections have more variety than most because they would not all be distributed by one furniture maker or fabric house.

LEFT
Marjatta Metsovaara, Finland
Relief Collection
wool, acrylic, polyamide
N. V. Albert van Havere, Belgium

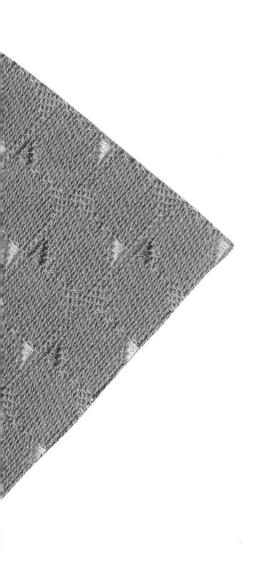

RIGHT
Designs from Katariina Metsovaara's Shape Collection illustrate how a designer can create a range compatible in both production and use, with jacquard patterning on one warp and the same weft yarns.

ABOVE
Bon-Bon
polyamide, polyester
jacquard double cloth
width: $54\frac{1}{2}$ in. (140 cm)
repeat: 7 in. (18 cm)

CENTER
Pallo
wool, cotton, polyamide
jacquard double cloth
width: $54\frac{1}{2}$ in. (140 cm)
repeat: $9\frac{3}{8}$ in. (24 cm)

BELOW
Pyramid
polyamide, polyester
jacquard double cloth
width: $54\frac{1}{2}$ in. (140 cm)
repeat: 10 in. (26 cm)
All: N. V. van Havere, Belgium

LEFT

Boris Kroll Design Studios, USA
*Highgate (top), †Rexford (left), *Bristol
(right)
wool, nylon
*jacquard damask, †satin
widths: 52 in. (132 cm)
repeats: 1 in. (0.6 cm); 8¾ (v), ×1½ in. (h)
(22 cm, 4 cm); 1⅝ in. (v), ¾ in. (h) (4 cm, 2 cm)
Boris Kroll Fabrics Inc., USA

RIGHT

*Here are damasks in several guises: "Troops" is
designed in small-scale geometrics for office
use; "Isaku" is first woven in black and white,
then overprinted. "Sotell" and "Eilau" show a
heavy coordinating tweed. "Spoleto" is a simple
satin damask, while the top one utilizes several
fabric structures in addition to satin. Its many
color tonalities are achieved through double
wefting (weaving with two weft colors
throughout).*

RIGHT (TOP TO BOTTOM)

Sotell, Eilau, Spoleto
wool, polyacryl
jacquard damask
Riedlinger Moebelstoffweberei, Germany

FAR RIGHT (ABOVE)

Elyse Wolford, USA
Troops
polished worsted
satin damask
width: 54 in. (137 cm)
Rudd Textiles International, USA

FAR RIGHT (BELOW)

Heinz Roentgen, Germany
Isaku
long staple cotton
jacquard satin damask, printed
width: 54½ in. (140 cm)
repeat: 31¼ in. (80 cm)
Nya Nordiska, Germany

It is interesting that the strongest trends in new
interior fabrics have as their common thread
the counterpoint of opposites. In sheers we see
this as a contrapuntal play of solid and void, or
opaque and translucent, or, in crêpe plissé, of
smooth against puckered. With prints, plays of
high gloss against matte are achieved through
lacquer printing.

In upholstery cloths the impulse to
counterpoint is even stronger. It is manifested
in the loop against cut pile of friezes, and in the
cut pile against ground cloth of voided velvets.
Even more popular is the juxtaposition of warp
and weft faces in damasks and one cloth against
another in double cloth. Damask furniture
coverings currently enjoy success not seen since
the Napoleonic era, when jacquard weaving was
new and figured silk damasks à la mode.
Today's damasks tend to be of long-staple
cotton or worsted fibers, both carded and
combed in the yarn-making phase and often
polished in finishing. While these are used for
both residences and offices, the neat, small-
scale patterns shown here were designed with
office use in mind. The coordinating pattern,
"Rexford," is not a damask but a satin with a
vertical stripe of black and white yarns twisted
together, or marled.

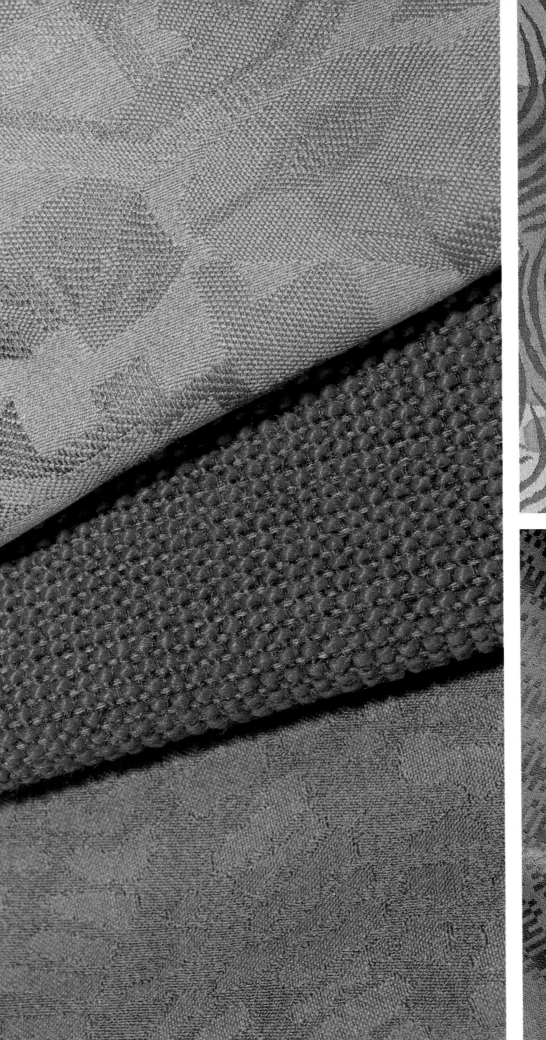

LEFT

The designer refers to this simply as a damask but it is much more than that: the ground is plain woven, and several small pattern weaves are included in the composition, in addition to the diagonals of two complex twills.

Manuel Canovas, France
Tcheou
rayon
jacquard damask
width: 51 in. (130 cm)
repeat: 32 in. (81.2 cm)
Manual Canovas. SA, France

RIGHT

For decades Boris Kroll has designed and produced jacquard damasks. This wood-grain pattern, shown with two coordinates, is one of the earliest and most popular: its "lazy" lines are without a specific period connotation and pattern matching is not necessary.

Boris Kroll, USA
Oak Park
cotton and rayon, Teflon finish
jacquard damask
width: 54 in. (137 cm)
repeat: $6\frac{11}{16}$ in. (h), $33\frac{3}{4}$ in. (v) (15 cm, 86 cm)
Boris Kroll Fabrics Inc., USA

TEXTURE   Whether an upholstery fabric is to be luxurious or practical, it should be chosen with a view to its tactile characteristics. Comfort is as important in upholstery as in apparel. A fabric's porosity, or the extent to which it (and its cushioning) permits the passage of air, is one factor in its comfort. Vinylized fabric, which has no porosity, not only is uncomfortable in itself – hot and sticky to the touch – but also causes clothing to go limp and become deeply creased. At the other extreme, prickly or scratchy fabrics are almost as irritating, especially in contact with bare arms or legs.

A common fault of modern upholstery fabrics is their neutral "hand" and monotonous surface. Too often indistinguishable from one another, they fail to supply the sensuous pleasure offered by such engaging textures as silk velvet, heavy satins, or ribbed or corded weaves.

Producers of upholstery fabric are increasingly sensitive to fashion cycles. Fabric types that dominate one decade tend to be eclipsed in the next. Because over the past decade, furniture coverings have become ever more sleek, we can expect soon to see the return of exaggerated Modernist textures. For the moment, however, sheen remains dominant. Nubby wools have been

For her recent collection for Knoll, Dana Romeis has designed several jacquard damasks that are not polished worsteds but of plied synthetic yarns. Their finish is smoother than the worsteds, the durability quite high, and the price low.

LEFT
Dana Romeis. USA
Pandora
rayon
weft striped damask
width: 54 in. (137 cm)
repeat: 7⅛ in. (17.8 cm)
Knoll Textiles. USA

RIGHT
Dana Romeis. USA
Cubis
rayon
damask
width: 54 in. (137 cm)
repeat: ¾ in. (1.9 cm)
Knoll Textiles. USA

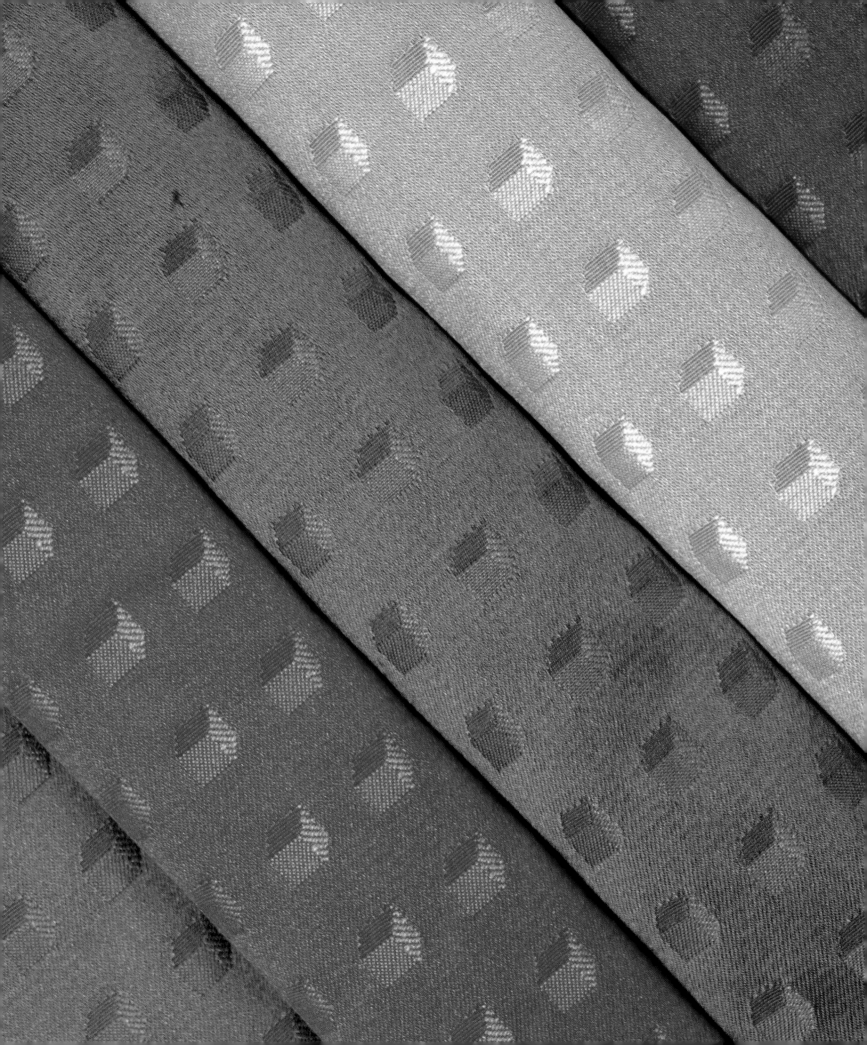

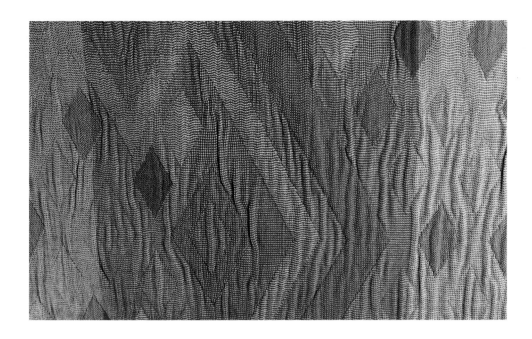

replaced by glossy worsteds calendered (pressed between rollers) for extra smoothness. As with draperies, satin weaves, damasks, and repps are in vogue; many of these are made of lustrous, light-refracting yarns and are polished after weaving, or given a moiré or chintz finish. The taste for refinement is also expressed, slightly differently, in soft pile fabrics such as velvets and chenilles. With the decline of Modernism, more patterned coverings are appearing — some so wild as to "camouflage" furniture. With this comes an occasional playfulness we haven't seen since the Youth Revolution of the 1960s.

Double cloths now are found in both dobby loom geometry, in designs such as checkerboards, and in fluid jacquard patterns. Matelasse double cloths are padded with "stuffer" yarns to resemble trapunto quilting, usually in jacquard patterns. Woven pleats are more often seen, so are figured friezes (or frisés) and velvets.

Of all pattern weaves, none are so newly popular as the jacquard "tapestries." At least four, and often as many as eight, sets of colored warps can be combined with two or more wefts to create an astonishing number of color tones. Using this method, shaded forms are easily achievable. An innovation of

LEFT

The cloth shown right utilizes the potential of different take-up and shrinkage in the yarns of the two cloths. Here, all of the face is puckered and all the back is smooth, but both surfaces could also be combined on each face. The color shift derives from a striped warp with wefts of alternating colors ("pick and pick"). This lightweight cloth is woven 112 in. (280 cm) wide for bedspreads.

Heinz Roentgen. Germany
Toronto
cotton. viscose. acrylic
double plain weave
width: 112 in. (280 cm)
repeat: 11¼–12 in. (29–31 cm)
Nya Nordiska. Germany

BELOW

From Scandinavia come several different approaches to double plain weave. As shown below, this technique can be used to juxtapose two pure colors, one on each face of the cloth, to form two correlated colorways from a single bolt (and sample).

Eva Larsson and Ann Larsson-Kjelin. Sweden
Zenith
wool
double plain weave
width: 58½ in. (150 cm)
Marks Pelle Vävare, Sweden

RIGHT

Double cloths can also be woven with "stuffer" yarns between the cloth layers to achieve the effect of padded quilting. The subtle changes in the peach-colored squares in "Labyrinth" is the result of plaiding the undercloth. The coordinating fabrics (Cherry, New York, and Candy) are cotton damasks.

W. Hall & M. Hjelm. Sweden
Labyrinth
cotton (face). polyester
double plain weave with stuffer yarns
width: 101¼ in. (260 cm)
repeat: 13¼ in. (34 cm)
Marks Pelle Vävare, Sweden

Quite different in scale and subject, both these damasks were inspired by the Vienna Secession at the turn of the century. "Sonnenaufgang" (Sunrise) is not only double wefted but subtly weft striped to achieve its pale polychrome coloration.

LEFT
Josef Hoffmann, Austria
Vineta
cotton, viscose
jacquard satin damask
width: 51 in. (130 cm)
repeat: $1\frac{1}{4}$ in. (v), $\frac{5}{8}$ in. (h) (3.1 cm, 1.5 cm)
Design Tex Fabrics, Inc., USA

RIGHT
Atelier Ruepp (1901), Austria
Sonnenaufgang
rayon, polyester
weft brocade
width: 51 in. (130 cm)
repeat: $19\frac{1}{2}$ in. (49.5 cm)
Joh. Backhausen, Austria; Ian Wall, Ltd., USA

the 1980s was to combine tapestry construction with a chenille weft yarn, or with areas of smooth ottoman repps. And because the yarns used are usually rather ordinary cotton, the price can be modest. So, of course, is the resistance to abrasion.

The novelty (or fancy) yarns so popular before and after the Second World War, then replaced with handspun yarns and slubby, machine-twisted homespuns, have begun to reappear – mostly in dull, nubby cottons. Bouclé yarns with their characteristic small loops will probably follow. We also see more use of moresque (jaspé) yarns – that is, those plied with two or more colors to achieve a barber's-pole spiralling stripe. Yarns printed or space-dyed in several colors along their length appear in both flat and pile fabrics.

Upholstery leathers, (shown on p. 166) often costly aniline-dyed, top-grain cowhides, are now more often used than they were formerly. Semi-aniline dyed leathers that have been sprayed or rubbed with pigment and a sealer as protection from soiling, are favored for commercial use. If these are tumbled to restore their softness, they can be quite attractive. Unlike the situation a few years ago, one now sees more luxury leathers in Britain and North America than in Continental Europe, where they have declined somewhat in popularity. Leather-like upholstery is seldom seen these days, except for the occasional use of Ultrasuede.

Renata Weisz has designed a collection entirely in polychrome double cloth. The plain coordinates are the iridescent bicolored single cloths found in these patterns.

Renata Weisz, Germany
Bonaventura Collection
cotton, chintzed
jacquard double plain weave
width: 54 in. (138 cm)
Zimmer and Rohde, Germany; Pontus, USA

RIGHT
Although double cloths are usually of plain weave, they need not be. This jacquard double cloth combines areas of plain weave with several stepped twills to achieve eight color shades. The warps are black and cerise; the wefts saffron and lavender blue. The small dots are to "tie down" the larger areas which would otherwise be too separate.

Anna Severinsson. Sweden
Chili
cotton
jacquard double cloth
width: 58½ in. (150 cm)
repeat: 3¼ in. (8 cm)
Kinnasand. Sweden

LEFT
"Arrow" is double plain weave; its many colors derive from striping the warp and weft of one cloth. The coordinating Roman-striped fabrics are wool-face satin.

Barbro Peterson. Sweden
Arrow
cotton, modacrylic
jacquard double plain weave
width: 58½ in. (150 cm)
repeat: 16¼ in. (42 cm)
Kinnasand. Sweden

LEFT
As evidenced in the many airline upholsteries originating in Switzerland, the possibilities for polychrome patterns of double cloth construction are many. As shown here, that the warp and weft colors are often not the same permits many possibilities for different crossings. Sometimes a third warp is used to increase their number still further.

Marjatta Metsovaara. Finland
Coupage (3262)
wool. polyamide. acrylic
double cloth
width: 53¾ in. (138 cm)
repeat: 18¼ in. (47 cm)
N. V. Albert Van Havere. Belgium

RIGHT
"Scrito" combines fine cotton with black slit film. The film gives the cloth an extremely high-gloss and slightly rippled surface.

Team Création Baumann. Switzerland
Scrito
cotton. polyester (film)
jacquard double plain weave
width: 54½ in. (140 cm)
repeat: 9¾ in. (25 cm)
Création Baumann. Switzerland

RIGHT
Another possibility with double-cloth structures is the pleat weave, which can have pleats as wide as desired. More often, the pleats are modest, rounded cords as those shown here. Two warp beams are always required; one remains taut, the other is released when the pleat area is woven. The pleats (or cords) may have "stuffer" weft yarns inside them. Those shown above in wool are prototypes designed on the loom by Hazel Fox of London. Those shown below, woven in cotton by Anne Beetz, include one of her rare uses of color.

LEFT
That the "pleats" can also take on other shapes or patterns is demonstrated by these sculpted cloths. The raised, braille-like relief is the more important for the white monochrome coloring.

Marjatta Metsovaara. Finland
Riti (ABOVE) Viiru (BELOW) (Relief Collection)
wool. polyamide. cotton
jacquard weave with supplementary warp
width(s): 54½ in. (140 cm)
repeat(s): 8 in.. 1¼ in. (20 cm. 3 cm)
N. V. Albert van Havere. Belgium

Over the years, Anne Beetz of Brussels has developed a unique personal aesthetic in furnishings fabrics. First, there is her reserve in avoiding color as such and all that is florid or demanding. Then there is the richness of the costly if simple yarns she uses, including understated metals as an integral aspect of the cloth. Her complete understanding of the loom gives her total command. Although she has always distributed from her atelier, her recent decision has been to design for larger mills with wider distribution.

LEFT (TOP TO BOTTOM)
Coup de pinceau
linen (face), cotton, polyester
jacquard frieze (cut and loop)
width: 51 in. (130 cm)
repeat: 25¼ in. (65 cm)

No. 614/644
cotton, rayon straw
jacquard double plain weave
width: 51 in. (130 cm)
repeat: 15½ in. (40 cm)

Sangle
linen (face) cotton and polyester
frieze (cut and loop)
width: 51 in. (130 cm)
repeat: 12½ in. (32 cm)

RIGHT (TOP TO BOTTOM)
No. 404
linen, cotton, silk
jacquard double plain weave
width: 51 in. (130 cm)
repeat: 6½ in. (17 cm)

No. 201/10
silk, cotton
double plain weave
width: 51 in. (130 cm)
repeat: 3 in. (8 cm)

No. 6004/60
cotton, silk
picquet weave
width: 54½ in. (140 cm)
repeat: 1½ in. (4 cm)

All: Anne Beetz, Belgium

Stripes – *the most elemental and universal form of patterning found throughout nature in rocks, foliage, and the animal world – are also the primary means of combining color in woven fabrics. Stripes can be vertical or horizontal, or both, in the case of checks or plaids, in two tones or many, in every scale and material. To a weaver the stripe is "free;" it takes no extra time, material, or device to produce, and can be combined with all other patterns.*

In both apparel and interiors, stripes are more used today than any time since the floral stripes of Louis XVI and the bolder, broad Roman stripes of the Empire style. Appearing in all forms and styles of furnishings, on every price level, on the terrace and in the ballroom, stripes are but the most visible aspect of a new urge to Classicism.

Traditionally, striped upholsteries have served decorators as a "bridge fabric," intermediate between two colors or between a dominant pattern and solid colors. While it is well known in apparel that vertical stripes are thinning and horizontal ones widening, this is too rarely considered in decorating. Proportions of furniture, windows, or rooms can be changed as easily. Sharp dark and light stripes can focus attention on a fine, small, chair. Broad, tone-on-tone color bands can diminish the apparent bulk of a too-large sofa or bed. Ceilings can be seemingly lowered or raised and disproportionate windows made to appear agreeable. Boldly striped carpets could be more often used to humanize vast public spaces, just as petite stripes and strias can be used to make rooms look larger.

Here is a sample of the range of simple stripes. The hanging on the left is horizontal, assymetric, finite in size, unique, and handwoven in wool as an exercise in color combination. Although using several scales and degrees of contrast, the Regatta Collection reflects tradition and formalism because of its common alternation of equal size bands.

RIGHT
Beatrijs Sterk. Holland
Summer Night in Finland
weft: wool; warp: cotton
plain weave
wallhanging 77¼ in.×17½ in. (198 cm×45 cm)
Beatrijs Sterk. Germany

FAR RIGHT
Osborne and Little. UK
Regatta Collection
cotton
screenprinting
width: 54½ in. (140 cm)
repeat(s): 5 in.–18 in. (13 cm–46 cm)
Stead McAlpine. UK

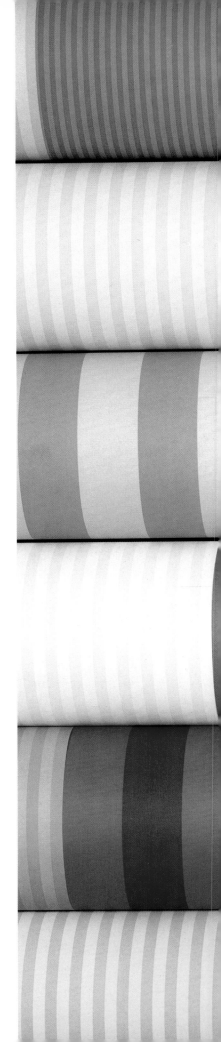

These warp stripes have in common their being
handwoven of cotton in south India. All are
warp-faced, with a rustic charm. All are
plainwoven, but the heavy repp of "Night and
Day" alternates two warp colors to achieve a
positive/negative reversal of the two cloth faces.

LEFT
Inger Elliott. USA
Night and Day Stripe
cotton
warp-face repp
width: 52 in. (133 cm)
repeat: 24¼ in. (61.6 cm)
China Seas Inc.. USA

RIGHT
Donghia Textile Design Studio. USA
Hapsburg
cotton
plain weave
width: 51 in. (130 cm)
repeat: 1 in. (2.5 cm)
Donghia Textiles. USA

BELOW
Donghia Textile Design Studio. USA
Lineage
cotton
plain weave
width: 51 in. (130 cm)
repeat(s): 1–7¾ in. (2.5–19.7 cm)
Donghia Textiles. USA

The urbanity of the Parisian, Manuel Canovas, is demonstrated in stripes of great sophistication in style and technique, always in combination with at least one other element. All are, in fact, warp-faced repp constructions. "Sinbad," the striped faille (a fine, warp-faced repp) is also printed with an animal pattern and given a moiré finish. Each broad band of the striped ottoman, "Carrosse," is enriched with stripes of three monochromatic colors. The heaviest construction, "Corindun," is of weft-striped, double-wefted damask diamonds set in a repp ground by means of a double weave. The styling and coloring are contemporary; the degree of intricacy speaks of another era.

DURABILITY   Several factors — all equally important — affect the life expectancy of upholstery. The first is the kind and amount of use. Even within the same room, one chair may be used ten times more than the others. The frequency and thoroughness of cleaning is a factor; so is the amount of light. Generally, fabrics that snag should be avoided, but even more vulnerable are those that slip, that is, in which the warp and weft yarns slide against each other. Even worse is seam slippage, or the gradual displacement of the seam from its correct position, which must be prevented, as it cannot be corrected. Backing the fabric with a coating of acrylic or latex will usually avert both slippage and fraying of cloth edges inside the cushion. Adequate seam allowance — at least half an inch, or one and a half centimeters — on an easily frayed fabric is also important.

Abrasion is so crucial a factor that it is treated in some detail under "Fabric Testing" in Section III. The result of one surface rubbing against another, abrasion is affected by the form and cushioning of the furniture, the expected use, and the fibers, yarns, construction, and finish of the fabric.

FAR LEFT
Sinbad
rayon face, cotton
printed faille, moiré finish
width: 48 in. (122 cm)
repeat: 13 in. (33.5 cm)

LEFT
Corindun
rayon face, cotton
jacquard double weave
width: 51 in. (130 cm)
repeat: $4\frac{1}{2}$ in. (11.4 cm)

RIGHT
Carrosse
rayon face, cotton
ottoman weave
width: 51 in. (130 cm)
repeat: $17\frac{1}{5}$ in. (44 cm)
All: Manuel Canovas, SA, France

Fabric arms are so vulnerable that furniture with upholstered arms may have half the life expectancy of seating without them. The next most vulnerable area is the top of the front cushion, especially if this is welted; like a car bumper, the raised welt takes the brunt of abuse. Cushions that can be turned or reversed are advantageous in this respect.

Fuzzing, caused by fibers working out of the fabric onto the surface, may be a problem. The fibers often roll into little balls, called pills. In some cases the pilling may be a temporary condition: if the fiber is wool or silk, the pills can usually be brushed away. The pilling of certain synthetic fibers is more serious, because they do not break away but cling tenaciously, absorbing dirt. Although testing for abrasion and pilling is useful and now common practice, it is successful only in reporting structured flaws of the original tested sample. The real criterion is, accurately, "Will it age graciously?" Upholstery without holes (or pills, or slippage) but battered, soiled, or crushed, is as sadly depressing as that with more serious damage.

Combinations of striping and ikat technique (tying and dyeing yarn to pattern) are common to all ikat cultures. The stripes of solid color are both enriching and, in terms of labor, gratuitous. The bold and quiescent vertical bands create a counterpoint common to all the resist patterns of Asia, which are designed to have a dramatic effect at a distance and yet have a personal scale when viewed close up.

The weft stripe, "Siam," combines ikat bands in high-value contrast to the bands of solid color. From the same collection by Jim Thompson Design Studio, Thailand, a vertical stripe, "Penang," incorporates bands of end-and-end texture. The close-value vertical stripe, "Silk Horizon," uses darker warp yarns to imply a rounded relief.

RIGHT
Jay Yang, USA (born Taiwan)
Obi
cotton
warp ikat
width: 54 in. (137 cm)
repeat: 27 in. (w), 25¼ in. (h) (68.6 cm, 64 cm)
Jay Yang Designs, Ltd., USA

FAR RIGHT (ABOVE)
Penang
silk
plain weave, ikat
width: 48 in. (122 cm)
repeat: 11½ in. (30 cm)

FAR RIGHT (CENTER)
Siam
silk
plain weave, weft ikat
width: 48 in. (122 cm)
repeat: 16 in. (h), 17¼ in. (v) (41 cm, 44 cm)

FAR RIGHT (BELOW)
Silk Horizon
silk
plain weave, ikat
width: 48 in. (122 cm)
repeat: 5¼ in. (13 cm)
All: Jim Thompson, Ltd., Thailand

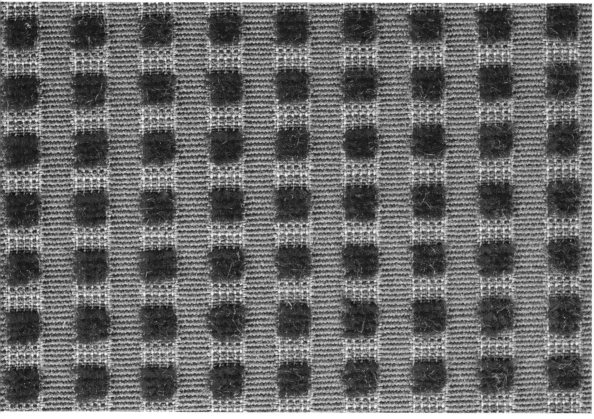

While stripes are almost always created with bands of color, they may also be a result of the weave. In the jacquard upholstery, vertical stripes in four color values further enliven a dynamic monochrome pattern.

The cut frieze below is banded with horizontal and vertical voids. In other versions of this cloth the pile bands are of several colors as well.

ABOVE
Esteban Figuerola, Spain
Los Armuras
double wefted damask
width: 54½ in. (140 cm)
repeat: 7½ in. (19 cm)
Esteban Figuerola, Spain

BELOW
Linda Thompson, USA
Clipstone
wool, rayon
voided cut frieze
width: 54 in. (137 cm)
Sunar Hauserman, USA

Crossing vertical and horizontal stripes to achieve a simple check is a natural outgrowth of the interlacing process that occurs in the oldest mattings ever found. The plaid, originally a term for cross-barred Scottish shoulder cloths, is generally used to describe complex or multicolor checks. Plaids can be "balanced," that is, with the same sequence in vertical and horizontal stripes, as in these replicas of Scottish tartans, or different, as in the printed plaid below.

ABOVE
Tricia Guild. UK
Great Expectations
cotton repp. chintzed
screenprinting
Tricia Guild Design Associates. Ltd.. UK

BELOW
Tartan Collection
rayon
twill
Brunschwig and Fils. USA

RIGHT
Linen furnishings in plain, dobby, and jacquard weaves are understated in pattern to play up the characteristic slubby texture of the linen fiber. They are used for all manner of furnishings, including wall coverings and nappery. (International Linen Promotion Commission, New York.)

LEFT
This group shows typical examples of classic neutral linen furnishings: from upper left, a whisper-thin gauze casement, a linen and wool blend upholstery, two black and natural tweeds in linen and cotton, a paper-backed "boiled" linen for walls, and a satin-striped silk and linen. (International Linen Promotion Commission, New York.)

BELOW LEFT
Three plainwoven and twilled checks in natural, boiled, and bleached linen are as generally applicable as they are inexpensive.

Hamilton Adams, USA

BELOW RIGHT
The German handweaver, Eva Kandlbinder, designed this handsome linen damask upholstery. The two color values lend the cloth an implied depth.

Eva Kandlbinder, Germany
(custom-design)
linen
damask
width: 54½ in. (140 cm)
repeat: 1½ in. (4 cm)
Eva Kandlbinder, Germany

In shifting from apparel, shoe, and accessory leathers to those for furnishings, Teddy and Arthur Edelman have retained a keen sense of style and an openness to broad, imaginative applications. As durable and soil resistant as their leather floor tiles (p. 195), are their hair-on cowhides (left). The ones shown here have been screenprinted with the patterns of endangered species. Edelman water buffalo hides (right) are heavily shrunken to achieve elasticity and a highly perceivable texture. (Teddy and Arthur Edelman, Ltd., USA)

Walls

Today, fabric is used on walls more than ever before and with good reason. The decline of craftsmanship in plastering, the ubiquitous use of monotonous (and vulnerable) painted plasterboard, the cost and rarity of stone or wood paneling all make lining rooms with fabric a natural choice. The fact that modern rooms tend to lack architectural detailing is another good reason; a wall fabric can instantly (but not permanently) give these look-alike spaces a distinctive character. The range of color, pattern, texture, and cost is almost limitless — from such simple textures as a silk tweed or polished linen to all manner of stripes, overscaled tapestries, or even mural effects. When I first advocated wall fabrics in the 1950s, it was because this seemed the kindest way to treat a patterned fabric, neither cutting it into upholstery shapes, nor hiding the pattern in drapery folds. Then, in the 1970s, the idea of covering walls with fabric received a further impetus when extra-wide looms made it possible to print length-for-width mural fabrics such as the one on p. 185 with repeats as large as 10 by 16 feet (3 by 4.8 meters).

Upholstered walls are so effective in absorbing sound that one wishes more restaurants would use them. In many open-plan offices they have proved their usefulness as sound barriers. By separating working areas with fabric-covered acoustic panels, office designers can accommodate more employees comfortably in a given space. These panels are also far more resistant than hard surfaces to knocks from office carts, and they require less in the way of cleaning. Then, too, vertical planes of fabric texture provide some relief to the necessarily gloss-hard horizontal planes of most office furniture.

When fabric first began to be applied to office partitions, in the 1960s, designers reveled in the potential for admixing brilliant colors and cheerful patterns, but when both became tiresome there was often no budget for replacing them; indeed, expansion often entailed adding more, to match the existing scheme. Today a more sober approach is adopted, using textured coverings in neutral or greyed colorings. Such neutral tones are particularly appropriate where fluorescent lighting (notoriously harsh on colors) is used.

The large scale, rich pattern, lush color, and texture of this wall fabric is appropriate as the principal decorative focus of a private dining room within a famous restaurant (Le Pavillion, Washington, D.C.). It supports the splendor of a luxuriously set table with an antique Japanese obi as its central runner. The chair fabric pattern is sufficiently quiescent to be subordinate to both. Here, the seamed and upholstered wall fabric covers only two niches on either side of the long table. Below it are built-in sideboards with storage particular to this special room.

Wall panel:
Terri Roese, USA
Iris
tussah silk
handpainted
width: 54 in. (137 cm)
repeat: 40 in. (102 cm)

Chair:
Vanessa
cotton
screenprint
Clarence House, USA
Interior design by James E. Peterson, USA, of Rita St. Clair Associates, Inc.

As fabric-covered office partitions have become more widespread, special "panel" fabrics have been developed specifically for this use (see p. 212). Typical panel fabrics are lighter in weight and less resistant to abrasion than upholstery fabrics, and are flame retardant. Their color tends to be subdued and lighter than middle value (and, of course, colorfast). They have enough texture to provide a restful contrast with hard and smooth work surfaces.

Panel fabrics must resist bruises and soiling and be sufficiently porous to work with the sound-absorbent battings (waddings) that fill the core of the panels. Whereas most furnishing fabrics are 40 to 54 inches (102 to 137 centimeters) wide, panel fabrics may be as wide as 72 inches (183 centimeters). Although most are distributed through office systems manufacturers, others are offered by fabric houses catering to the office furniture market. In some cases, notably executive floors, where a measure of luxury may be considered appropriate, more distinctive upholstery fabrics are sometimes used on panels, such as those dividing private secretaries' work stations.

Because the widespread use of wall fabrics is a recent development, fire codes for wall fabric in many regions are more stringent than for upholstery or drapery. There is no good reason for this: fabric applied to a wall is more difficult to ignite than the same fabric hung loosely, and it will also burn more slowly. Still, local codes must be adhered to when selecting the fabric. Some untreated cloths pass these tests; others can be treated with a flame-retardant chemical to comply with the codes. If this is necessary, ask to have a sample treated; if the luster or color is too diminished, consider another cloth.

The four walls of a large New York drawing room have been gently draped with panels of heavy handwoven cotton, with natural selvages exposed. Such a treatment unifies the interior walls and windows of an older building. It could also cover walls and windows without harming unwanted paneling or plaster work in need of costly renovation. Together with the natural texture of the coir (coconut fiber) floor tiles, the wall panels provide quiet support for a highly individual collection of art and furniture. (Interior design by Paul Mayan, USA.)

Drapery:
Custom fabric
cotton
plain weave
Isabel Scott, USA
Carpet:
Felix Ruckstuhl, Switzerland
Tahiti
coir and sisal
loop pile
size: 19½×19½ in. (50 cm×50 cm)
Ruckstuhl, Switzerland; Larsen Carpet, USA

Shown left are a variety of woven, natural-fiber wall fabrics, in the widest range of applications. The OJVM series was power woven in five colorings, given a flame-retardant finish, then backed with a peelable, self-adhesive backing paper. The edges are trimmed (pre-cut) and ready to hang by anyone, including home owners. Below it is a handwoven Philippine wall fabric bold in texture and with natural variations in size and coloring of materials. It, too, is paper-backed for direct paste-up, then trimmed on the wall.

ABOVE
OJVM Design Studio, Belgium
OJVM Series 200
cotton, linen
dobby weave
width: 59 in. (150 cm)
O. J. Vanmaele, Belgium

BELOW
Docey Lewis, USA
Mayon Texture
cotton, Lurex, hand-knotted abaca
plain weave
width: 36 in. (92 cm)
Silk Dynasty, Inc., USA

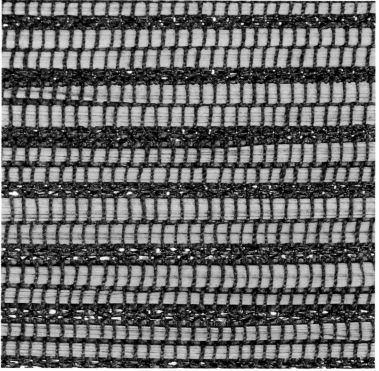

RIGHT
This treatment, for walls and ceiling of a round country sitting room, is the simplest, in that the fabric is neither finished, paper-backed, nor pasted-up. Instead, hundreds of yards of handwoven tussah silk were shirred top and bottom as they were stapled. A baseboard covers the lower staples, and a large, self-covered welt the upper ones, where the wall and ceiling meet. The fabric above the several French windows was shirred over pre-cut plywood panels. The deep, oversized daybeds are covered with a heavier natural silk that has been channel quilted. The many cushions are also in natural tones, so that the overall effect is rustic and quiet, but not without comfort.

Wall fabric:
Bengal
silk
plain weave
width: 48 in. (122 cm)
Jack Lenor Larsen, USA

Upholstery:
Shan
silk
plain weave
width: 40 in. (102 cm)
Jack Lenor Larsen, USA

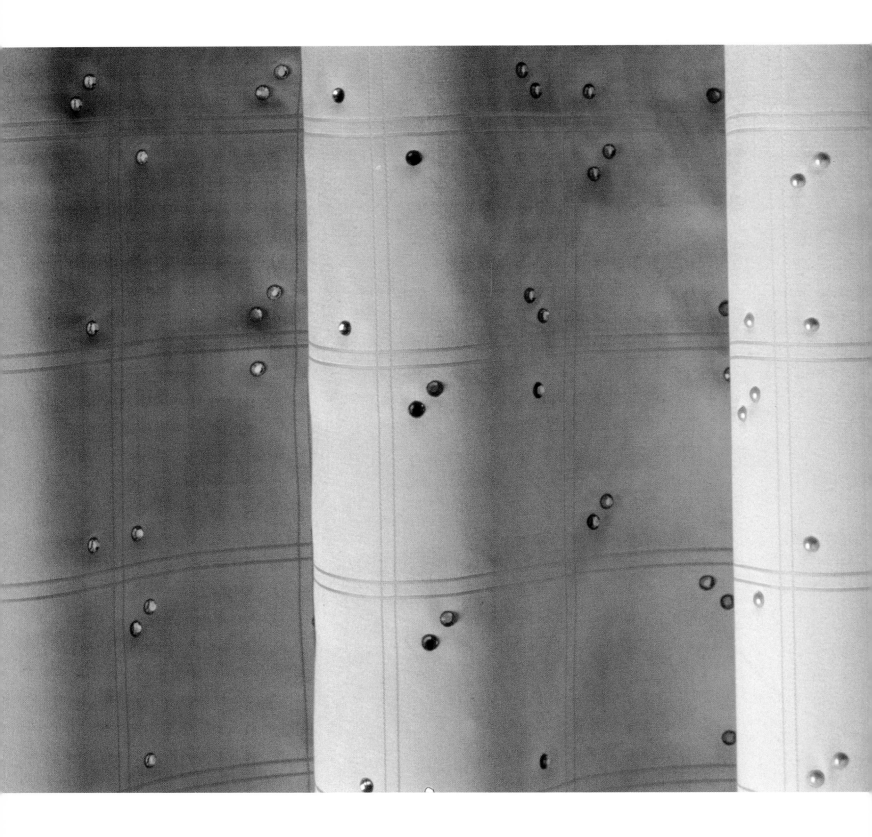

METHODS OF APPLYING FABRIC Upholstering walls has become simpler in recent years, as most localities now have competent installers. The power staple gun makes the work relatively fast and uniform. There are also several reliable patented devices for clipping fabrics onto a metal or plastic strip which has been tacked to the wall. For padding, battings of various thicknesses and fiber types are readily available. Alternatively, the fabric can simply be pasted to a flat, unpadded wall.

The costliest, most luxurious method is to seam the cloth into wall-sized panels, then stretch it as a single unit over the batting, previously attached to the wall, and blind tack it in place. This is also the most practical method, as the fabric can easily be moved or temporarily removed for immersion cleaning. This fact was dramatically demonstrated when, just before the opening of a major museum gallery, a furnace exploded, sending black soot over every surface. The costly, handwoven fabric panels were taken down, dry-cleaned and reinstalled within two days. If the fabric had been simply pasted to the walls, it would have needed to be totally replaced, perhaps after a long wait for delivery.

Yet another method, wrapping fabric over padded, pre-cut wooden or Homosote panels, is, of course, easier than the seamed method and, in some situations, just as suitable. These panels can have an architectonic quality if they are rounded to a slight curve at the corners and hung with a quarter-inch (half-centimeter) reveal, or shadow line, between them.

In many cases, however, budget limitations will necessitate simply pasting the fabric in place. In the best paste-up installations paste is rolled onto the wall, the fabric pressed onto it, and the edges trimmed with a rotary blade, as for untrimmed wallpaper. As the fabric, slightly dampened by the paste, becomes more resilient, it can be stretched or contracted at the installer's will — a great advantage in matching patterns.

When installers demand fabrics as easy to put up as wallpaper, a fabric with a paper or resin backing can be used. Backing, however, may be

Although this fabric can, as shown, be used as drapery, it is probably even more spectacular as a wall covering. The rhinestone-emblazoned silk will pick up sunrays by day and glamorous highlights after dark.

Gretchen Bellinger. USA
Diva
silk, studded with rhinestones
width: 57 in. (145 cm)
repeat: 2⅜ in. (6 cm)
Gretchen Bellinger Inc., USA

problematic because of the tendency of backed fabrics to end up off-grain. Most often this takes the form of "bowing:" the center of a panel is shorter or longer than the sides. Because there is no way to correct this, it must be avoided. The best prevention is to buy from a responsible supplier. Better yet, so as not to be caught between installer, backer, and fabric house, let the installer make the purchase. Another potential problem is that of side match. Many fabrics, even seemingly plain ones, have subtle bars or irregularities in the weft, which will not match from one panel to another. If there are enough seams, and one has a modicum of tolerance, the repeated "mis-match" effect may be as acceptable as it is in wood or stone.

Here are two contemporary wall treatments, both with soothing horizontal lines. Both are washable, and designed for the economy of paste-up application without problems of side match. The pleated material is a heavy paper with a satiny, pearlized colorant protected by a thin lamination of vinyl film. The pleats are secured by a plain paper glued to the back.

The sculptured surface of the wall shown right (detail, left) is created with deposit printing. The luminous ridges are raised and rounded, and the valleys are covered thinly with vinyl to show off the weave of the canvas ground.

LEFT AND RIGHT
Night Hawk
vinyl, cotton canvas
deposit printing
Art People, USA

FAR LEFT
Scott Simon, USA
Wall Pleats
paper, vinyl
pleating, lamination
width: 30 in. (76 cm)
repeat: 1 in. (2.5 cm)
Innovations, USA

SPECIAL EFFECTS   Fabric shirred over a rod at top and bottom can (if properly installed) be one of the most luxurious of wall treatments. Because triple fullness is required, this effect is not cheap; however, a costly fabric may not be necessary. And where an alternative treatment would entail re-plastering – as in an old building with irregular walls – the cost of covering the walls with gathered fabrics can be relatively low. A similar treatment was used to cover the walls of a drawing room in a distinguished old apartment in New York. Panels of heavy, hand-woven cotton, left unseamed with selvages exposed, were loosely hung from the ceiling cove around all four walls. The effect is so striking that no-one would guess that this was also an economy to avoid having to restore the walls themselves. And what marvelous walls these panels create – offering subtle intonations of the fabric structure, superb sound control, and a lively, if neutral, background for the works of art suspended in front of them (see p. 171).

The direction of textured wall coverings is finally moving away from imitations of natural fibers such as woven grass cloth, toward the machine aesthetic of these crisp reliefs. The design seen here is a heavy embossed vinyl. Those shown right are in the tradition of nineteenth-century anaglyptics, which were heavy, embossed papers, often imitating hand-tooled Spanish leather. They were painted, then highlighted with a second color or metallic gilt. The fine line patterns shown here are not embossed but deposit printed with a durable foam. After installation they can be painted any color. Full-gloss lacquers are often used, and glazing with a second shade is quite possible.

LEFT
Patty Madden, USA
Rivets
embossed vinyl
width: 36 in. (92 cm)
repeat: 2 in. (5 cm)
Innovations, USA

RIGHT
Ozamu, Veliki, Tepa, Onda
laminated paper
foam deposit printing
Zimmer and Rohde, Germany; Pontus, USA

As with other aspects of interior design, the most successful fabric wall treatments are often the most unexpected. The effect may be lavish or spartan, but in some way it should take chances. One might, for example, cover the walls with a rich Lyon silk and drape the windows with plain cotton crash: each fabric enhances the other. Such contrast is especially desirable if the room, or the furniture in it, lacks its own character.

Many fabric collections have coordinating wallpapers, with the same pattern screened on both cloth and paper. This is no mean trick to achieve. The cloth must necessarily be as structureless as the paper; the colorants must be pigment, rather than dyes; and the control from one production lot to another (often in separate plants) must be meticulous. It can be, and is, done successfully – sometimes with charm – and at several price levels. Correlated collections, in which fabric and paper are stylistically related, but not identical, are easier to produce and permit more options.

Another relatively new idea is the use of carpets on walls. The wide variety available at all prices is one factor in this trend; others include the

LEFT
The early nineteenth-century campaign chair is an example of reversible covers. Being two-sided, the loose pad can as easily have different colors and patterns on each side. The reverse of this one is a solid khaki silk. The same principle can be used for chair pads, cushions, bedspreads, and so on.

Upholstery:
Jack Lenor Larsen. USA
Laotian Ikat
silk
plain woven. weft ikat
width: 40 in. (102 cm)
repeat: 12 in. (31 cm)
Jack Lenor Larsen. USA

RIGHT
Walls of fabric on sliding doors (fusuma), which are ubiquitous in Japan, could be used more extensively elsewhere. The effect is so much "quieter" than exposed shelves of books or objects. The author's apartment has 52 of them: over closets, library shelves, windows, and between rooms, and, as here, collections can be revealed one section at a time. To balance the tension of stretching cloth on such light-weight frames there must be material on both sides. The Japanese use lining stock for the back side, but, as shown here, two "front" fabrics are as easy to fabricate. Then, in five minutes, the whole decor of a room can be changed.

Panel fabric:
Larsen Design Studio. USA
Bengal
tussah silk
plain weave
width: 48 in. (122 cm)
Jack Lenor Larsen. USA

obvious tactile appeal of carpet, its sound-absorbent properties, and its low maintenance requirements. But most designers now feel that pile carpets on the wall are appropriate only in certain public places such as cinema lobbies, bars, and student lounges. A frequent mistake is to cover floors, walls, and occasionally seating, with the same carpet. This may have a dramatic effect when newly installed, but a year later the varying ravages of dirt and wear will have been disastrous. Flat carpets of sisal and coir (coconut fiber) seem much more appropriate for walls. Their clearly visible weave is architectonic, and in an office it gives welcome relief from a sea of monotonous, smooth surfaces. These carpets, too, need only low maintenance, usually vacuuming is sufficient.

The sliding door, opposite, is covered with a plain woven scrim of bleached paper yarn. The waffle-weave scrim (detail, above), is highly suitable as a special grille cloth.

Ritva Routila. Woodnotes. Finland.

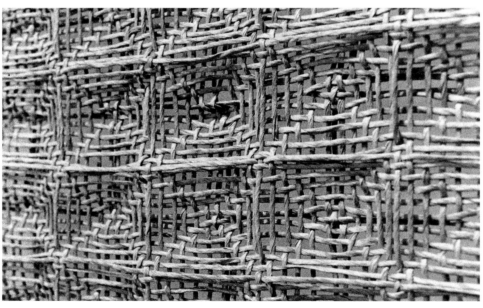

Finland, with some of the largest cotton mills in Europe, had no cotton yarns to weave with during the Second World War. The paper yarns from native forests substituted for cotton were so unpopular with weavers that they were abandoned as soon as imported cotton was available again. Now, the artist-weaver, Ritva Routila, has been experimenting with paper yarns as a favored material. She sees it as *lightweight, lint-free, and inexpensive, with the agreeable aesthetic of reed and raffia. She has knit paper sheers with the look of chain mail and woven it in all manner of structures. Most often she weaves flat, dense mattings as table mats, or as an alternative to the woven rag rugs so popular in Finland. Elsewhere these are used as wallcoverings. Shown left, is a variety of mattings for walls or floors.*

Shown left are two extremely durable plain-woven wall fabrics designed for paste-up application. The upper one is of tightly twisted natural sisal. The one below is woven with a slit and folded plastic film in 106 stocked colors. The silky-smooth surface resists every kind of abuse, including stains and flame.

Raja
sisal
plain weave
width: 78 in. (200 cm)
Ruckstuhl AG. Switzerland; Larsen Carpet.
USA

Vi Becker. Bob Goldman. USA
Striae (a Xorel Fabric Wallcovering)
polypropelene
plain weave
width: 52 in. (133 cm)
Carnegie Fabrics, USA

WALL HANGINGS   The broad category of textiles known as wall hangings embraces tapestries, embroideries, quilts, and various other kinds of woven, knotted and tufted structures. A fuller discussion of these can be found in my books, *Beyond Craft: The Art Fabric* and *The Art Fabric: Mainstream*, both written in collaboration with Mildred Constantine, and listed in the bibliography. The fabrics in this category are essentially works of art, rather than wall coverings. Their potential for strong, direct, even poetic, expressions of form, color, highlight and shadow, makes them ideal means of enlivening spaces begging for just these qualities. Some wall hangings are sculptural, incorporating high relief or worked in the full round. The problem with regard to these is how to protect the work during shipment and installation and, later, how to keep it clean. For this reason, flat fabric hangings, including tapestries,

For this dramatic wall fabric an extremely wide cloth of cotton and linen was printed with an enormous silk screen (120 in.×200 in.; 300 cm×500 cm), then turned length-for-width to be stretched on the wall without seams. The sofa fabric is a handwoven silk ikat.

Walls:
Larsen Design Studio, USA
Pantheon
cotton and linen
screenprint
Jack Lenor Larsen. USA

Upholstery:
Jack Lenor Larsen. USA
Laotian Ikat
(details as p. 180)
Interior: Suzy Langlois, Paris

have recently regained favor over the three-dimensional ones, which enjoyed such great popularity in the 1970s.

Whether flat or sculptural, wall hangings have a broader appeal than other forms of modern art. The tactile appeal of the materials used, and the intriguing, often innovative, demonstration of traditional craft processes are especially welcome in areas devoid of such expression. And although the cost per square foot is commensurately high, compared with other textiles, a relatively small work may fill — aesthetically, if not literally — a considerable volume of space.

LEFT
Helena Hernmarck. USA (born Sweden)
Sailing (for Federal Reserve Bank. Boston)
wool
tapestry
width: 240 in. (610 cm)
height: 132 in. (335 cm)
Helena Hernmarck Tapestries Inc.. USA

ABOVE
Monika Speyer. Germany
Tumbling Blocks
acid-dyed pongee silk
hexagonal plaiting
width: 72⅛ in. (185 cm)
length: 87¾ in. (225 cm)
Monica Speyer. Germany

Floors

When we speak of "floor fabrics," of course, we mean primarily rugs and carpets. (Other fabric treatments, such as painted canvas floor cloths, or the practice of pasting a fabric print to a floor, then protecting it with varnish, have limited application.) Like other types of furnishing fabric, carpets and rugs serve the purpose of making interiors more comfortable, inviting and individual.

It is worthwhile remembering that carpets and other fabrics are, in many cases, constructed using the same, or similar, materials and processes. For a fabric designer, the fact that Wilton carpets, jacquard friezes, and terry towelling share the same basic methodology is a stimulus to creativity. Concepts and devices from one can be carried over to the other.

This structural overlap is well illustrated by the story of a group of men in rural Georgia who, back in the 1930s, pitched in to help their wives make some candlewick bedspreads. Growing weary of the monotonous process of hand-tufting, they devised a machine that would do several rows simultaneously. At about the same time, they hit on the idea of making carpets in this simple way. Today, tufting accounts for more than ninety per cent of all carpets made, becoming a multi-billion-dollar industry.

Warren Platner's renovation of the lobby of New York's Pan Am Building included the installation of this floral patterned, wool Axminster carpet. Its sunny, light coloring, chosen to offset the low levels of natural light at the bottom of a city canyon, has presented maintenance problems. The scale of the pattern repeat (60 in.×36 in., 152 cm×91 cm) is in keeping with the monumental space.

carpet and interior design:
Warren Platner Associates, USA

TYPES OF CARPET   Carpets and rugs are a subject in their own right, and many books have been written about them. Only the basic types are identified here, and their main characteristics touched upon. Although in the Oriental rug trade the word "carpet" is used for knotted pile rugs and "rug" for flat woven ones (usually kelims), "carpet" in the West implies wall-to-wall (or fitted) soft floor coverings. Rugs are subdivided into area rugs, which relate to a furniture grouping; room-size rugs, which nearly fill a room, and simply "rugs" for sizes in between. Especially in country houses, runners — often in flat weaves — are still found in halls and on stairs. Fortunately, scatter rugs (those little rugs that clutter and skid) have nearly disappeared.

The general trend has been to lower, denser piles with the smoothness of velvet rather than the shags and plushes of previous decades. Jacquard patterns, often in large repeats, are Wilton-loom woven as carpeting and bordered rugs. More of these appear in all types of interiors, in both modern and traditional styles. Only hotels seem to favor bordered Axminster carpets for their lobbies and corridors. New sophistication in patterning devices for tufted carpets are producing a broad spectrum of new patterns, many of them the small and neat, computer-generated geometrics now more often seen on office floors. Similar graphics, also in new types of nylon (which do not glint and are resistant to built-up static) are produced by Milliken's patented Militron process, in which hundreds of hypodermic needles, controlled by a computer, injection-dye carpet pile yarns down to a considerable depth. A number of these patterns are available as carpet tiles, as well as broadloom carpets.

At the other end of the spectrum are the tapestry-woven dhurrie rugs, handwoven in Pakistan and India in wool or tightly twisted cotton twine. These are so popular internationally as to be widely available, in many qualities.

Once considered a luxury, wall-to-wall carpeting has become so ubiquitous that room-size rugs are now often favored for such important areas

The redesign of a large banking hall included carpeting to muffle footsteps and absorb ambient sound. The other objectives were to make the room less awesome to staff and visitors, and more contemporary in spirit.

A large-scale wool Wilton pattern ("Metropolis") was laid asymmetrically to define traffic areas and to balance the rich ceiling detail. The carpet also defines work areas; its shaded neutral tones are dirt-hiding, and either it or the coordinating solid carpet ("Gibraltar") can be replaced separately.

Metropolis
wool Wilton
jacquard weave

Gibraltar
loop velvet
Both: Larsen Carpet, USA

Union Commerce Bank, Cleveland
Architect, Julian Abbott

as executive offices, boardrooms, and elegant living and dining rooms. These rugs are often recessed, so as to be level with the surrounding marble or hardwood floor. This luxurious custom treatment is, to be sure, costly — though less expensive than laying a rug over luxury flooring. The hidden cost is maintenance; for each surface must be cleaned separately — and rather carefully. If possible, the rug should be delivered to the site in advance, so that the workmen can make the recess to its exact measurements.

A somewhat more practical custom effect – often found in hotels, for example – is carpet with a border where it meets the walls. This has the advantage of appearing to have been designed for the space, but, like ordinary carpeting, is easily maintained. The same borders can be stitched to rugs, which gives both producer and distributor a secondary market.

Carpet tiles, especially loose-lay ones (so heavily backed that they need not be glued down), are coming into wider use – and with good reason. They can be repositioned to distribute the wear caused by traffic patterns, or to hide a tile that is hopelessly stained. For those offices with communications conduits under the floor, carpet tiles may be the only sensible solution. They are also useful in furnishing the upper floors of tall buildings, where delivering heavy, cumbersome rolls of broadloom may present a problem. This is particularly true in the case of refurbishing, when construction cranes and

Although the pattern of too many printed carpets tends to feel on the carpet rather than within it, this one – with a shaded stripe motif both lighter and darker than the ground – is successful. It also provides a type of patterning not possible with woven or tufted processes.

Elizabeth Strassle. Switzerland
Mira-Dessine 40
polyamide
printed. cut pile
width: 180 in. (457 cm)
repeat: 36 in. (v). 38 in. (h) (92 cm. 97 cm)
Mira X AG. Switzerland

elevators used to lift the original carpets are no longer available. Carpet tiles are available in wool, nylon, wool/nylon blends, and coir (coconut fiber). A fine example of the latter is shown overleaf.

In a lobby, a high traffic area such as that around the reception desk takes more abuse than other areas. Specifying a different floor covering, or simply color, makes it possible to replace the worn covering without attempting the impossible task of matching a new carpet to an older one. The same principle could be applied in the home, in open-plan rooms, which include both traffic lanes and seating areas.

Obviously, the floor is the largest single furnished area in a room; and the larger the room, the more important the floor becomes. Apart from lighting, no design element is as crucial: it affects all other aspects of the interior. The interrelationship of lighting and floor covering has an even greater bearing on the ambience of a room. For example, a prominent banking house on New York's Fifth Avenue recently chose traditional grandeur for its new premises. The palatially scaled ground floor was endowed with Georgian detailing, crystal chandeliers — and a red carpet. Bathed in a myriad down-lights from high above, this vast expanse of red suffused the entire room with a lurid pink glow, quite out of keeping with the desired effect.

The relationship between lighting and pattern can be even trickier than that between lighting and solid color. In the late 1970s the distinguished architect I. M. Pei commissioned the Larsen Studio to design a patterned carpet for the auditorium of the John Hancock Building, in Boston. When his office approved a sample with brutal color contrasts, they were called for an explanation. Once it was pointed out that the theater lights would normally be down to five foot candles, and that in such dim lighting any softer coloring would simply not "read," production went ahead. Slightly different considerations apply in the case of the candlelit restaurant, where a carpet with a rich pattern may be desirable not only for aesthetic reasons, but also for its ability to conceal stains.

Largely through the pioneering efforts of the Swiss firm, Ruckstuhl, sisal and coir (coconut fiber) carpets are more popular today than ever before. They are available in several widths of carpeting, as bound rugs, and (with a heavy backing) as carpet tiles – all in a range of colors and weaves.

From top left: Raja sisal rug
Tahiti coir carpet tile (19½ in. × 19½ in.; 50 cm × 50 cm).
Chevron (sisal and coir), Tonga coir rug
Ruckstuhl AG, Switzerland; Larsen Carpet, USA

FIBER AND DURABILITY

The fiber industry's quest for ever more durable carpet fibers is a major one: only the clothing industry uses up a comparable amount of fiber. For those who can afford it, wool continues to be preferred. It gives good service and cleans exceedingly well. The best carpet wools once came from the tough desert sheep of Central Asia. Unfortunately these are now an endangered species – living and breeding as they do in areas of frequent conflict. In the past, wars between Japan and China, civil war in China and the long period of isolation which followed have prevented proper breeding and production from these sheep.

Although wool is not so resistant to abrasion as nylon (in the same construction and density), wool and wool blends (usually eighty per cent wool/twenty per cent nylon) have a larger market segment than a decade ago. These are often selected for executive or residential areas, or, in heavier weights, for lobbies and other public spaces.

At last, nylon carpet yarns have improved. Problems with static electricity and dirt retention have, in most cases, been resolved. The newest generation of nylon is without the terrible "glint" it used to have; and it feels good. As a result, nylon now leads in carpet fibers.

Along with the quality of the fiber, the amount of it is crucial to a carpet's durability. The depth of the pile is not as important as its *face weight* – that is, the density of fiber in the pile. If asked, sales staff will disclose (if

floor tiles
leather
sizes: 2 in. × 8 in. (5 cm × 20 cm); 4 in. × 4 in. (10 cm × 10 cm); 8 in. × 8 in. (20 cm × 20 cm); 12 in. × 12 in. (30 cm × 30 cm); 18 in. × 18 in. (45 cm × 45 cm).
Teddy and Arthur Edelman, Limited, USA

sometimes reluctantly) the face weight of a carpet. In terms of durability carpets are often divided into four grades. Grade One is intended for residential, or domestic, use; Grade Two, for normal contract (commercial) use; Grade Three, for such public areas as lobbies, where face weight is especially important; and Grade Four, for stairs, offices containing chairs with casters, and institutions. Many Grade Four carpets have an uncut loop pile for greater resilience.

The recent trend of using contract carpets in private houses has much to commend it. By and large, the two are not so dissimilar as suggested by their quite separate modes of distribution. Many of the solid-colored and small-figured carpets designed for offices are perfectly suitable for residential use and expand the range of contemporary styles available; and the more durable carpet tile lines are a good choice for home owners who prefer to lay the carpet themselves. Conversely, for years the hotel industry has used residential grades for such light-use areas as hotel bedrooms. The designer lines and custom carpet trade have always catered to the top end of both the residential and contract markets.

For informal rooms there is a growing fashion for flat, tapestry-woven kelims and dhurries in both cotton and wool, for rag rugs and other handwovens, mostly from the developing countries. Texture-rich, hard-fiber rugs and carpets are more popular in the West than ever before. Among the fibers used are rush, seagrass and sisal; but coir carpets are taking the lead because, of all hard fibers, coir best withstands the ravages of dry heat. A newcomer is maize, or cornhusks; the Chinese braid, then stitch this attractive, ivory-coloured fiber into neat area rugs.

The bold jacquard pattern of this wool Wilton carpet helps to make a large private plane more personal. Its monochrome tones unify the several cabins and set the palette for the interior scheme.

Interior design by Joy Guernsey Designs. USA.

Jenny Foley. UK and Larsen Design Studio. USA
Radiance
wool
Wilton weave
width: 144 in. (365 cm)
repeat: 36 in. (h). 48 in. (v) (92 cm. 122 cm)
Larsen Carpet. USA

Linens and Accessories

Of all interior fabrics, "domestics," or bed and bath linens, are the most fashion-responsive; that is, they are often of high style and in high-key colors. Major showings occur twice a year, and lines may change radically from one season to the next. This is a large market, led by increasingly large firms. Distribution is far-flung, with the leading products readily available in most towns and cities. The turnover is rapid, especially in patterned goods. Because of this, budgets for advertising and sales promotion are so high as to promote sales in a short time frame.

BED AND BATH   Because bath and bed linens are intended for private rooms, the customer is often more adventurous in selecting them than when buying furnishings for more public areas of the home. Then, too, the risk is smaller; mistakes can be kept in the linen closet. Although these linens are still not as integrated into furnishing schemes as other fabrics (blankets and pillowcases are usually covered with a spread; the bathroom door is usually closed), the trend is towards coordinated collections, sometimes including rugs and draperies. With larger bedrooms and bathrooms (and more of the latter), these spaces have acquired new status. A bedroom is no longer just a place to sleep and dress, but a personal haven containing, possibly, such amenities as television, a breakfast bar, a writing table, upholstered furniture, and sometimes fitness equipment as well. It may have architectural features, such as a fireplace or French doors leading to a garden. A bathroom, too, may include extra furniture and accessories, such as plants and pictures, to make it more inviting. Such rooms merit linens that are stylish as well as serviceable.

At one time, the choice in sheets was between muslin and percale cotton, usually white. Then there was a period of wrinkle-free polyester-cotton blends, most often printed. These came at higher prices (and higher markups) but offered reduced ironing and extended life. Today even blends are available in several counts (threads per inch, or centimeter), and fine-count cottons are returning, albeit at extravagant prices. The growing demand for fine linens

A sense of luxury is given an open-bed suite in which each cover is framed with related patterns. The number of pillow shapes and sizes and the sheet-covered duvet are Continental influences. Note the festooned treatment of both windows and walls.

Perry Ellis, USA
Palmyre Garlands
cotton, polyester
printed
Martex, West Point Pepperell, Inc., USA

may be attributable to increasing travel. One of the pleasures of staying at a luxury hotel is that of sliding into a bed made up with crisp, smooth linen sheets. Perhaps more people would even choose linen for their homes, were it not for this fabric's notorious tendency to crease, making it necessary to start with fresh sheets each day.

A Continental fashion which has spread to Britain and, recently, to North America, is the "open bed" – that is, one without a spread and with pillows and other linens exposed. In place of a spread and blankets there is a *duvet* (a feather bed slipped into a case made of sheeting) or simply a blanket in a cover, plus coordinating sheets, several pillows, and a dust ruffle (valance). These linens may be quite sumptuous. The idea behind the open bed is that it should look ready to enter – not unmade (making it consists merely of fluffing up the pillows and duvet). The effect of eliminating a spread is to focus more attention on the other linens, and to increase the budget allowed for them.

RIGHT
The many moods of Martex bed and bath ensembles span the pattern influences of several centuries. The trend is toward luxury, with ever finer counts of cloth, often in 100 per cent combed cotton, more sophisticated print techniques to allow fine line work, half-tone shading, and more colors.

ABOVE (LEFT)
Perry Ellis. USA
Boulevard
printed cotton

ABOVE RIGHT
Martex Design Studio. USA
Solid Colors
printed cotton

BELOW (LEFT)
Martex Design Studio. USA
Manette
printed cotton

BELOW (RIGHT)
Liberty of London. UK
Eden Hall
printed cotton

All: Martex. West Point Pepperell. Inc.. USA.

A printed patchwork pattern is both contemporary in spirit and compatible with antique furnishings.

Marras
cotton
screenprinting
Marimekko. Finland

Now under new leadership, the Helsinki firm of Marimekko continues its cutting-edge design program. Printing methods are not as simplistic as formerly. A wider range of both ground cloths and more applications for them have been sought, including those for bed and bath and as table linens. The cotton screen-prints shown here, however, are furnishings fabrics from the Sydantalvi Collection by the Japanese designer, Fujiwo Ishimoto.

Panel:
Fujiwo Ishimoto, Japan
Marras
cotton
resist printing
width: 58½ in. (150 cm)
repeat: 54½ in. (140 cm)
Marimekko, Finland

Tablecloth:
Fujiwo Ishimoto, Japan
Uoma (see p. 81)

Napkins:
Fujiwo Ishimoto, Japan
Ti'hku
cotton, linen
discharge printing
width: 58½ in. (150 cm)
repeat: 9¾ in. (24.8 cm)
Marimekko, Finland

With sheets now readily available in more interesting styles — and in such generous widths — there are many possibilities of using them for draperies, slipcovers, skirted tables, and even upholstered walls. Both the manufacturers and the magazines encourage this; stores, however, have shown less initiative in promoting it. As a result some of the newest bed and bath collections include made-up draperies, tablecloths, shower curtains and cushions.

Towels have changed less in style than other bed and bath linens, though jacquards are less popular than a few years ago. Luxurious, solid-color qualities, often in larger than standard sizes, dominate the world market. Particularly in Japan and Scandinavia we see trends to clean-cut contemporary styling, often in long, shaggy terrycloth pile. The greatest change in bath linens from one season to the next is in the rapidly changing colors.

Recently, both the Japanese and the Scandinavians have woven terry towels with long shaggy pile and a look of being "thirsty." Usually these are in multicolored patterns. (The towels shown here are 19½ in.×39 in. (50 cm×100 cm) and 27¾ in.×58½ in. (70 cm×150 cm).)

FAR LEFT
Liisa Torsti. Finland
Kongo
cotton
jacquard and terrycloth
Finlayson. Finland

LEFT
Markku Piri. Finland
Kuu (The Moon)
cotton
dobby woven terrycloth
Finlayson. Finland

RIGHT
Liisa Torsti. Finland
Keidas (Oasis)
cotton
jacquard. terrycloth
Finlayson. Finland

OVERLEAF
The Swedish firm, Marks Pelle Vävare, has pioneered the development of sheared terrycloth blankets. As shown, the process provides many possibilities for color and patterning. The cloth is also lightweight and easily washable. These can serve as bedspreads as well, being especially useful for such casual quarters as students' rooms.

LEFT TO RIGHT
Amadeus. Allegro. Cielo. Jazz
cotton
sheared terrycloth. jacquard weave
width(s): 62½ in. (160 cm)
repeat(s): 13½ in.–101½ in. (35 cm–260 cm)
Marks Pelle Vävare. Sweden

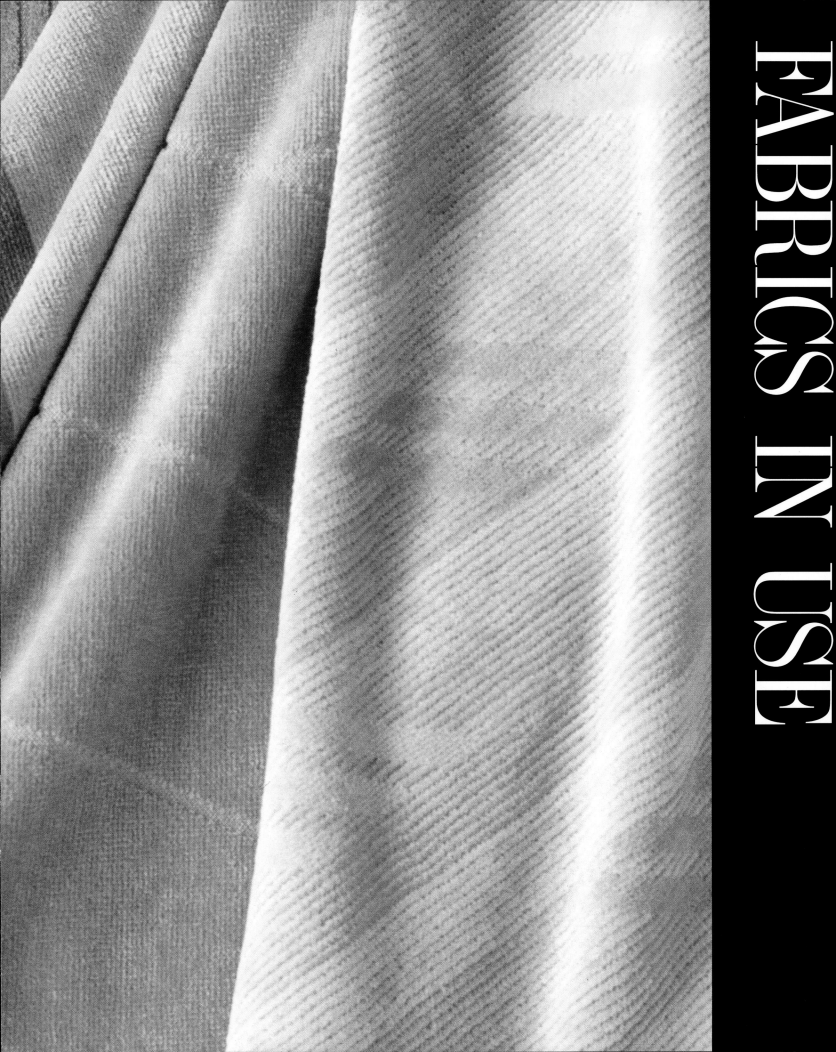

FABRICS IN USE

Developments in Contract Design

Was there ever a term with so many different meanings as "contract"? The clumsy synonym, "non-residential" is too negative a way of describing this multifarious segment of the furnishings market to get us very far. Even to those much involved with this field, the term "contract" is misleading. When a client asks, "Is this fabric suitable for contract?" is he thinking of resplendent executive suites, with generous funding and meticulous maintenance, or of the stringent budget, high performance, and low maintenance required for institutional use?

Fortunately, this problem is being resolved by subdividing the area into such categories as "executive," "general office," "institutional," "health care," and "hospitality," which may be further subdivided according to quality, indicated by such terms as "top," "moderate," and "low budget." Design for stores, banks, showrooms, and the like may include several levels of budget, use, and maintenance. Even within a single large store, for example, the fashion salons and executive offices would be treated differently from other areas.

Whereas chairs in private homes may receive only occasional use, and be treated with fastidious care, most office and lobby chairs are used hard and often. Fabrics used for them must therefore be tough and easily cleaned. Style, too, is subject to certain restrictions. Although pattern is now more often seen in office furnishing than formerly, the norm is an unobtrusive, business-like appearance. Fabrics for office boardrooms are suitably formal and sedate. Corporate dining rooms, for all staff levels, may have a more relaxed aspect.

Left, four of these chintz-covered panels slide and stack to open this space to an adjoining sitting room.

Interior design by Rita St. Clair Associates, USA
Fabrics: Karl Mann Associates, USA

The idea here is to provide a contrast with work spaces, including lower or higher light levels, as appropriate, more color, and sometimes pattern.

"Hospitality" or "soft contract," which includes catering businesses such as hotels, restaurants and also clubs, is a newly differentiated market and one of the fastest growing ones. Two factors have led to a raising of design standards in this area. First, hotel and restaurant owners have recently learned that profit in the luxury end of the business can be as secure as that at the lower end (and the job more interesting). Thus, they are more willing to upgrade their enterprises. Moreover, high-quality design is a reliable, non-fluctuating ingredient in the "package" offered by an establishment – unlike service, which can slip on occasion. A customer receiving an enormous bill on top of indifferent service (and possibly a meal that failed to live up to the Michelin star) may be more tolerant of these shortcomings if the surroundings, at least, are comfortable and luxurious.

In a sense, of course, there always was a contract market: but until the late 1950s it did not seem to have much to do with design, or at least with

RIGHT
More than most architects, Warren Platner has always used wall fabric importantly and dramatically, as visual incident and for acoustical correction. In this conference/dining room, for Wright, Morris and Arthur, Attorneys, Columbus, Ohio, some of the panels of softly upholstered fabric open to reveal a chalk board, projection screen, and other items.

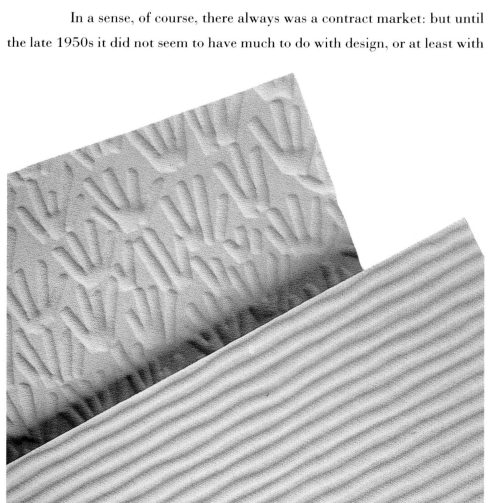

LEFT
These panel fabrics are dimensional embossings on a layered and laminated panel fabric. The aim of the furnishing is to minimize distraction and provide relief in the suggestion of natural forms.

Textura
Westinghouse Furniture Systems, USA

modern design. Put another way, it did not form so large a segment of the total furnishings market; it was not so visible or so much publicized as to be considered the separate, and in some cases dominant, furnishings market it is today. So important is the contract market that it now profoundly influences the design of most furnishing fabrics. Even those fabrics developed strictly for residential use may utilize fibers, yarns, or methodology geared to contract furnishings.

What brought about this situation, of course, was not just the office-building boom of the post-war era, or modern design becoming the corporate style. Rather, the nature of the business changed in these years. Mills, factories, and trading firms merged into giant conglomerates needing headquarters buildings – often in major cities. Large segments of the work force moved from blue- to white-collar jobs, and needed new kinds of work spaces, with incentives to stay in them. These interiors had to express not only the prestige of a corporation, but also that of its executives. Spacious and luxurious suites were intended to convey an image of supremely efficient, confident, and loyal decision-makers totally committed to success – and, in fact, to foster such a spirit. As this ethos extended downward into the middle management and general office staff levels, it created a bonanza for the furnishing design industry. Although the many advances in communication and computers reduced staff numbers, specialized skills were needed, with high pay scales. Expert supervision was required; so were systemic office furnishings that could accommodate rapidly changing work methods.

Systems furniture, first developed by Knoll International and The Herman Miller Company in the 1950s and 60s met these requirements so successfully that these systems became in themselves a major industry. Often, all of the furnishings for an entire floor, a building, or a far-flung organization – including most fabrics – would come from a single supplier. This enterprise was a jackpot worth considerable research, development, testing, and careful marketing and pricing.

The walls of an office reception room are paneled with a striped silk fabric. The linen bows attached to it provide a lively shadow pattern especially welcome in space without windows.

MGIC Investment Corp., Milwaukee, WI
Interior design by Warren Platner Associates

The foyer of the newly renovated Rainbow Room high above New York at Rockefeller Center contrasts bold jacquard patterns on a curvilinear fabric wall and a Wilton carpet. Largely because of the contrast in texture and value, this unlikely combination succeeds.

Wall:
Larsen Design Studio, USA
Cabaret
nylon, wool filament and cotton
jacquard double plain weave
Jack Lenor Larsen, USA
Carpet:
Larsen Design Studio, USA
(custom design)
Wool
Wilton
Larsen Carpet, USA

Interior design by Hugh Hardy of Hardy, Holtzman and Pheiffer Associates.

Optimizing the working conditions in small, semi-private work stations within vast office floors is no mean feat. Most have little or no natural light; ambient sound is never quite absent, and every visual incident is impersonal, if not inhuman. As an antidote, panel fabrics to cover walls have been given much consideration. These provide texture and softness to contrast with the hard, monotonous plastic laminates used for horizontal surfaces.

The jacquard-woven panel fabrics above are texture patterns, using dark and light yarns to imply textural relief.

Steelcase, USA

Distribution of Furnishing Fabrics

Although top-quality furnishings (including the fabrics in this book) are sold in different ways around the world, they fall into two general marketing systems. The distribution model used in Britain and North America is basically "to the trade only" – that is, through showrooms and sales networks catering to architects, interior designers, and others who specify furnishings. Purchase orders may be placed by these firms, or by a wholesaling furniture dealer, a corporate buying office, a furniture manufacturer, or a fabric workroom.

Some of these fabrics may also be available through department or specialty stores, upholsterers, or decorating shops, who will usually keep books of samples, from which customers can order. A few shops will stock a limited range of fine fabrics. Unless the shop has a workroom, however, there is the potential problem of a customer's not knowing how much to order or where to have it made up. Fabrics produced in larger volume, for wider distribution, are sold through department and furniture stores, specialty shops, and upholsterers. Upholstered furniture, window treatments, rugs, and carpets are offered on both an as-shown and a special-order basis.

The Continental approach is quite different: there are no regional showrooms for the top-quality lines, nor, in some cases, even national ones. International furnishing fairs are crucial to distribution. Usually held annually, such large fairs as Heimtex (held in January, in Frankfurt), Star (May, in Milan), the Cologne Furniture Fair (January), and the Scandinavian Furniture Fair (May, in Copenhagen), offer every aspect of furnishings, at all price levels. Others, such as Decorex (held in September, in London), and Atmosphere (January, alternately in Paris and Frankfurt) offer luxury furnishings of the sort shown here. These fairs give ample opportunity for designers, distributors, manufacturers and the press to get an overview of the market, as well as to meet with each other. Consumer sales are through stores specializing in either contemporary or traditional interior furnishings. Many of these are quite large, with a full range of furniture and fabrics, plus rugs, carpets, and accessories, at a range of prices. They can afford to sample such a vast variety of goods partly

Decorative printed fabrics are important to two small bedrooms shown here and on p. 208. This one, at a corporate conference center, combines the same patterns for the quilted spread and the boxed valance. The upholstered headboard was framed with picture molding, then attached to the wall.

Interior design by Rita St. Clair Associates, USA
Fabrics: Clarence House, USA

because they also supply local architects and interior designers, who specify furnishings to be purchased and installed by the store itself (a relationship similar to physicians writing prescriptions to be supplied by chemists). Most of these stores employ their own interior designers as well.

Cosmopolitan centers such as London, Paris, and the French Riviera support many interior designers, showrooms, and shops that specialize in furniture, accessories, or fabrics alone. Outside Europe and North America one tends to find some combination of the two basic distribution models. For instance, Japanese producers and importers have showrooms selling both to stores and through designers and architects doing contract work. Many interior design firms in Australasia have international sample libraries, and either they or the client may arrange for the importation of the chosen furnishings.

This mammoth fringed, velvet drapery reinforces the Regency style of a renovated hotel. At times, it also serves to close off the mezzanine café from the lobby below. (Peabody Court Hotel, Baltimore, Maryland – interior design by Rita St. Clair Associates)

Drapery: Stroheim and Romann. USA

Fringe: Brunschwig and Fils. USA

Ordering Furnishing Fabrics

Apart from furniture sold "as shown" (that is, identical in every respect to the floor models) or curtains purchased ready-made, most furnishing purchases involve an order. This purchase order should contain complete, detailed specifications. Such written specifications ensure that everyone concerned — customer, and retailer or manufacturer — knows exactly what has been ordered, and help prevent unpleasant surprises ("But I thought the stripes would be vertical," for example.) They are particularly important where two or more vendors are involved — as when upholstery materials come from one source and furniture from another (called COM, "customer's own material" or COL, "customer's own leather"). The same would be true when purchased fabric is sent to a workroom to be made into draperies or bedspreads. The transaction becomes more complex if the fabric must also be sent out for such a special finish as backing or flame retardancy; but here again, clear specifications should prevent mishaps or delays. Should an error be made, these specifications will indicate who is at fault.

Among the specifications that may need to be included on the purchase order are the following:

FACE   Even though both sides of a fabric may look totally alike, all fabrics have a face, or a right side, which is the one rolled towards the inside of the fabric bolt. In furnishing fabrics, face is important, because these cloths are often mended to one side, or given such a special finish as calendering or acrylic backing. Fabrics described as reversible — that is, with a different pattern or color on each face — are mended on both sides; therefore, specification as to which face is to be exposed is even more important.

DIRECTION   Window and wall fabrics are almost invariably run vertically. In direction patterns such as botanicals, the correct direction may be so obvious as to prevent error. If the pattern is subtle or the decision arbitrary, the top should be indicated, either verbally as "upholster with the pile slanting down,"

or by indicating with a sample or swatch attached to the order, as to which is the desired direction. Cut-pile fabrics such as velvet, and napped fabrics such as suede cloth are normally run with the pile running downward or, on horizontal planes, forward, although for heightened color richness velvets are sometimes hung with the pile slanting up.

Upholstery fabrics are often turned ninety degrees (or railroaded) to make pattern matching easier, to eliminate seams, or simply to comply with factory standards. If the fabric is directional, it is necessary to specify how it should be applied.

LENGTHS   Window and wall fabrics should always be ordered in terms of the number of lengths (or cuts) required. This allows the shipping room to send

Two views of the famous Ritz Bar at the old Ritz Carlton Hotel in Boston show upholstery and wall fabrics reversed from one room to another. The banquettes covered in the same upholstery fabric as the wall provide a sense of spacious serenity.

Interior design by Benjamin Baldwin. USA

that many flaw-free lengths. Failure to make this specification often delays shipment. For upholstery fabrics, which will almost always be cut into smaller pieces, allowances are made for flaws not cut out of the goods shipped. For instance, an 18-yard (16.5 meter) order with two minor flaws may be shipped as 18½ yards (17 meters). Flaws are usually tagged at the selvage.

PATTERN PLACEMENT   Many fabrics, including striped ones, have a motif so dominant that it should be centered on chairs and sofa cushions. Other patterns, however, are designed so as to have no obvious repeat. Unless such a fabric is specified to "fall at will," there is a good chance that the upholsterer will center it anyway, which will result in unnecessary monotony and a great waste of fabric. If sofa cushions are to match pattern, extra fabric may be required. The same is true of side-matching fabric pattern repeats for windows and walls. Here, panels may require as much as one full repeat of additional yardage.

Other drapery specifications would include width and type of hems and headings, types of pleat, and distance between hem and floor or sill. If lining is specified, also indicate the width of the turnback. Upholstery specifications often indicate the kind and amount of cushioning, and any use of welts and buttons. All specifications to workrooms indicate where to send any remaining fabric.

Many decorative fabrics which are not pre-shrunk can be used for washable tablecloths, pillowcases and slipcovers if they are thoroughly washed before make up. If the label does not indicate washability, test a small sample first.

A chair, table and pretty fabrics offset the essential hygienic considerations of a hospital room in Columbia Hospital for Women, Washington, D.C. Using the same soft print for window and cubical curtains, provides a unified sense of design.

Interior design by Malino and Metcalf, USA
Curtain fabric: Maharam, USA

Finally, a fabric purchase order should include the fabric's name, number, and color, and should indicate who should be contacted if a question arises concerning such matters as color match or delayed delivery. Fabric shipments going out for special finishes or make-up should be marked for whose account and for which pieces they are intended.

DURABILITY In the context of upholstery fabrics, durability almost always concerns resistance to abrasion. The abrasion tests described below are primarily aimed at determining when the yarns of the cloth first begin to break. Color loss, fuzzing, and pilling may also be noted in these tests. If reported accurately the tests give a reliable index of a fabric's durability in a given set of conditions. In relation to actual use, however, test results are less relevant. Here one needs, above all, to know what kind of use will be applied to the fabric. Why is such durability required? And at what loss in terms of style or cost? A desk chair that is used most of the day, every day, will put any fabric to the ultimate test; but even here, other factors will be at work. As with all seating, the type of frame is a crucial factor, along with the manner in which the chair is sprung and padded: a loose spring or frame corner abrading the fabric from within is disastrous. A welt at the upper front edge of the seat cushion may wear through several times faster than any other area. A chair without arms, or with wooden arms will need to be reupholstered much later than one on which cloth- or leather-covered arms which must bear the brunt of rubbing elbows and sweaty palms.

Since the introduction of down-like synthetic fiber fillings, the terms "soft cushion upholstery fabric," or, "for light upholstery," have been used to describe those cloths which are only moderately durable. Many prints and cotton damasks fall into this category; so do most fabrics described as dual-purpose. Loose cushions can be reversed and rotated to even out both wear and soil. Secondary covers over the arms also help, but they should be put on *after* the upholstered fabric is worn or soiled.

FIBER AND STRUCTURE   As described below, heat and light adversely affect both fibers and dyestuffs; so does low or extremely high humidity. But none of these factors affects a fabric's relative durability as much as does its construction. In the past three decades, all design professionals have tended to speak too much in terms of fiber content, too little of yarn and fabric structure. General fiber characteristics have meaning only if all other factors (including the use of the fabric) are similar; but they rarely are. A fair comparison of wool and silk upholsteries, for instance, would be of equal quality, appropriate fibers in each, both spun and plied to a similar extent, and comparably woven, finished, and (possibly) backed.

Within each generic fiber group are many grades of fiber at very different prices. For example, within the generic category of wool (even "pure new wool") are many varieties, including breed of sheep, grade of fiber, and the amount and quality of processing. One must also consider the amount of fiber: all other factors being equal, a heavy, densely woven cloth will wear better than a thinner one of the same fiber.

ABRASION TESTING   The simplest and fastest of the various abrasion testing methods is the TeledyneTaber Abraser 5130, which employs a weight fitted with an emery cloth-abradent which is applied in a circular motion. The test is quick and the equipment so simple that it is widely distributed. The results, however, may have little relevance to actual use.

The Martindale Wear and Abrasion Test is the most accurate measure of durability, because it best simulates normal wear. Normal wear is caused by friction between clothing (apparel fabric) and upholstery fabric. The Martindale abradent is a wool cloth, foam backed (representing the apparel cloth). Because this abradent is moved against the upholstery fabric in a multidirectional pattern, the method simultaneously tests both warp and weft. Yet another test, the Wyzenbeek, uses a method of rolling an abradent of either wire mesh or cotton duck back and forth. But because the results may be for either warp or weft they tend to be misleading.

Comparative testing of the Martindale and Wyzenbeek methods has been done to evaluate the reliability of the Martindale system results. The Martindale method has provided the results most consistent with experience. Extensively used in Europe, it is the standard adopted by the International Wool Secretariat.

The Martindale abrasion resistance is measured in terms of the number of rubs that can be administered without noticeable wear. A rating comparison with the Wyzenbeek is as follows:

Rating	Martindale	Wyzenbeek (with wire mesh; double rubs)
light upholstery	10,000	
medium or residential	20,000	up to 15,000
contract or heavy-duty	40,000	15,000+

These tests are useful only if combined with common sense. Because all of us have so much more experience with clothing, we tend to be wiser in our garment selection. We learn to use durable, easily cleaned cloths for active sportswear, but do not limit ourselves to these for evening dress. In other words, there is a time and place, and purpose, for fragile fabrics — even as upholsteries. Loose cushions or pads which can be re-covered without removing the furniture might be one, pillows another, and seldom-used seating or rooms, a third.

COLOR FASTNESS   The color of all fabrics changes with time. Light (especially sunlight), heat, dust, gas fumes, and abrasion are factors in this change. Some colors soften rather agreeably, some change cast, and a few bleached bast fibers (such as linen, sisal, and coir), and certain leathers may darken.

Most of today's washable fabrics are wash-fast, although bath and table linens that are laundered frequently will in time show signs of color loss, especially if bleaches are used. *Crocking* or dye loss through excess dyestuff rubbing off onto another material, is also an infrequent problem. Testing for wet and dry crocking is performed by a simple device which rubs white cotton over the surface. Anyone can simulate the test sufficiently to identify this fault. Crocking almost never changes the appearance of the fabric itself, unlike *color abrasion*, which is the perceptible loss of color through rubbing. The most frequent offenders are fabrics printed with thick or light-colored pigments, and those made from yarns so dense that they resist complete penetration by the dye. When the surface fibers wear off, undyed areas appear. Cloth woven from bast fibers may be problematic; so may the edges and welts of such densely woven cottons as canvas and duck.

All the potential faults just described are dwarfed by the major challenge of achieving superior light-fastness — in each production lot and for all applications. Luxury fabrics done in small lots and incorporating innovations beyond the range of the standard product are more prone to fading than those that are mass-produced. Intense blues and greens and fuchsia pinks still tend to give the greatest problems. Common sense in selection, sensitive placement, and protection from direct sunlight and intense artificial light remain advisable precautions when using these fabrics.

Most producers frequently check dyed goods for colorfastness (although seldom for each dye lot). The standard for Western Europe is the xenon fadeometer, on a scale of 1−8, rather than that of 1−5 used in the United States. The higher the rating number, the better the light fastness. Ratings of 6 and above are considered good. The tests used in the United States for color fastness to light and crocking include those listed on the following pages.

COLORFASTNESS TO LIGHT

AATCC 16A (carbon arc)

Rated by amount of fading.

Measured in 20 hour intervals up to 60 hours.

Test criteria

    1   Class 5 = no fading

    2   Class 4 = slight fading

    3   Class 3 = noticeable fading

    4   Class 2 = considerable fading

    5   Class 1 = excessive fading

AATCC 16E–82 (xenon fadeometer)

Rated by amount of color alteration.
Measured in 20 hour intervals up to 60 hours.

Test criteria

    1   Class 5 = negligible or no color alteration

    2   Class 4 = slight color alteration

    3   Class 3 = noticeable color alteration

    4   Class 2 = considerable color alteration

    5   Class 1 = much color alteration

COLORFASTNESS TO CROCKING

AATCC 8

Both wet and dry procedures.

Wet and dry have same rating system, measured by amount of crocking.

Test criteria

    1   Class 5 = negligible crocking = excellent

    2   Class 4 = slight crocking = good

3   Class 3 = noticeable crocking = fair

4   Class 2 = considerable crocking = poor

5   Class 1 = excessive crocking

Special finishes are those done to order at the customer's request. These include several kinds of back coatings. Acrylic and latex coatings, which reduce slippage and fraying, are often applied to upholstery fabrics as part of the production process. Dual-purpose fabrics, especially silk ones, are generally not given a backing, but some fabric houses will do this as a special service, at a slight extra cost. Others will refer their client to a finisher, who will perform the service, then send the fabric on for make-up. Special backings can also be applied to fabrics that are to be pasted to walls; however, this may cause some distortion of the fabric, especially in the case of paper backings. Delicate fabrics are sometimes laminated to a cotton muslin or, now more frequently, to a cotton tricot, or "stocking backing." This provides some stability and abrasion resistance, and helps prevent fraying.

There are now several types of treatment for flame retardance, to meet almost every fire code (see Fire Codes, page 232). Some of these are minimal, designed to assist a fabric which otherwise almost meets the code. Others are durable to many cleanings. The choice of treatment in a given case will depend on the code's requirements, the fabric selected, and the fabric's appearance after treatment. Fabrics with high percentages of polyester or modacrylic may be difficult to treat. Some treated silks and most chenille fabrics may change in color or texture. In these cases, an enquiry should be made before specification and purchase. If the seller does not have experience with treated fabrics of this type, a sample should be tested.

Unlike apparel fabrics, furnishing fabrics are almost always permanently mothproof. The mothproofing treatment should protect against weevil infestation as well. But if a label on wool or mohair fabric does not state that the fabric is mothproof, an inquiry should be made. Nowadays the most likely offenders would be exotic hand-weaves and fur fabrics acquired in Third World countries or from craft shops. Often only partially scoured (that is, washed during manufacturing), these cloths contain oily fibers irresistible to insects; they must be treated.

In climates where mold and mildew are common, an antibacterial protective finish may be desirable. These are readily applied by the same special finisher, without affecting the appearance of the cloth.

Over the last quarter-century, a number of treatments have been developed to inhibit the ravages of dirt. Silicon treatments to reduce water-borne stains came first, then the 3M Scotchgard treatment for oil-borne stains. Most recently, DuPont's Teflon protection promises a barrier to both water- and oil-borne stains and soiling from dry atmospheric particles. In addition to these internationally-distributed finishing solutions, there are now franchised services for protecting and maintaining all interior fabrics, including carpets and wall coverings.

Without knowing specific requirements, one hesitates to recommend any one of them. Most have considerable strengths, if some weaknesses. Those who have used them claim that some treated fabrics are more difficult to clean thoroughly than those not treated. Other treatments may repel dirt for only a limited time. Perhaps the drawback to such treatments is that they may encourage the use of a too-delicate fabric or too-light color where a firmer, darker fabric would be more appropriate.

Flat fabrics such as printed cotton sheeting are sometimes coated and laminated to make them so impervious to dirt as to require only damp sponging. This treatment multiplies the range of patterns available for the walls of powder rooms, for example, or eating places. Another use is for tablecloths for families with young children. Because these surfaces have no porosity they are not suitable for seating. Such fabrics can also be laminated to rigid sheets of acrylic and so be given all of the practicality of plastic laminates. Uses for laminated fabric include wall paneling and café table tops.

Although not strictly a finish, quilting is a technique that enhances the durability of fabric, along with its tactile appeal. Today the range of quilted effects has been increased by a wider variety of batting (wadding) materials and thicknesses and by faster and more flexible sewing machines. Machine quilting can be worked to a set repertoire of such existing patterns as stripes, diamonds, and hexagons. Much more costly, single-needle, hand-guided machine quilting can be as intricate as one's purse can buy. Usually such quilting follows a pattern or is *vermicelli*, an abstract squiggle pattern. The higher cost of this fabric can be mitigated by using it only in small amounts, such as on the cushions of lounge furniture upholstered in the same fabric.

Fire Codes

Bibliography

Fire codes are determined by individual State and local governments. In general, there are code requirements for curtains and draperies, wallcoverings, and upholstery. Below are given some of the specific tests which are generally accepted in the USA.

Curtains and Drapery

National Fire Prevention Association (NFPA) 701 Small Scale
Samples are ignited and measured for both afterflame and length of char of the warp and of the filling. The maximum afterflame for any one specimen is 2.0 seconds. The length of char maximum is dependent upon the weight of the fabric, with a maximum value for both the average and the individual specimens. Residues which drip or break cannot continue to flame after reaching the test chamber floor.

NFPA 701 Large Scale
Samples are ignited and measured for afterflame, drippings and char length of both the warp and the filling. The afterflame is not to exceed 2.0 seconds. Material which breaks or drips cannot continue to flame after reaching the test chamber floor. If the test is done on a flat sample, the char length maximum is 10.0 inches, on a folded sample, the maximum is 35.0 inches.

Federal Aviation Authority (FAA) 25.853(b) Vertical
Three samples are ignited. To pass, the average afterflame may not exceed 15.0 seconds, the drippings must not continue to flame longer than an average of 5.0 seconds after falling, and the average burn length must not exceed 8.0 inches.

California Bill 117, Section E
Both the face and the back of the samples are subjected to direct flame impingement for one second. If the fabric ignites, it does not meet the standard.

Wallcoverings

American Society of Testing Materials (ASTM) 84 (also known as the Tunnel Test)
This measures the rate of burning, after lighting, through horizontal flame spread and smoke development. The smoke development value must be less than 450. A flame spread value of 0–25 is Class A, 26–75 is Class B, 76–200 is Class C, above 200 is not rated.

NFPA 701 Small Scale (See Curtains and Drapery)

Upholstery

California Bulletin 117, Section E (See Curtains and Drapery)

FAA 25.833(a) Horizontal
The requirement is that the samples have a burn rate that does not exceed 4.0 inches per minute.

ASTM 84 (See Wallcoverings)

FAA 25.853(b) Vertical (See Curtains and Drapery)

Upholstered Furniture Action Council (UFAC) Classification (Cigarette Ignition)
Classification is determined by the vertical char and the ignition of the substrate. If the samples produce a char less than 1.75 inches and if the substrate does not ignite, it is a Class I fabric. If the char of any one specimen is equal to or greater than 1.75 inches, or if the substrate ignites, it is a Class II fabric.

In the UK, the British Standards Institute publishes guidelines for industry on all aspects of consumer safety covered by legislation. The following BSI codes set down standards for fire safety tests for furnishing fabric applications:

Floorcoverings
BS 4790   Method for determination of the effects of a small source of ignition on textile floor coverings (hot metal nut method).

Curtains, draperies, window blinds
BS 5438   Methods of test for flammability of vertically oriented textile fabrics and fabric assemblies subjected to a small igniting flame.

BS 5867   Specifications for fabrics for curtains and drapes: Part 2 Flammability requirements – performance criteria for the tests in BS 5438.

Upholstery
BS 5852   Methods of test for the ignitability of upholstered composites for seating by smokers' materials (Part 1) and flaming sources (Part 2).

Albers, Anni, *Anni Albers On Weaving*, Wesleyan University Press, USA, 1965.

Albers, Anni, *Anni Albers On Designing*, Pellango Press, USA, 1959.

Constantine, Mildred and Larsen, Jack Lenor, *Beyond Craft: The Art Fabric*, Van Nostrand Reinhold, Inc., New York, 1972.

Constantine, Mildred and Larsen, Jack Lenor, *The Art Fabric: Mainstream*, Van Nostrand Reinhold, Inc., New York, 1980.

Design in America – The Cranbrook Vision 1925–1950, Harry N. Abrams Inc., New York, 1983.

Design Since 1945, Philadelphia Museum of Art, 1983.

Emery, Irene, *The Primary Structures of Fabrics*, The Textile Museum, Washington, D.C., 1980.

Encyclopedia of Textiles, Editors of American Fabrics Magazine, Doric Publishing Company, USA, 1960 (1st edition).

Encyclopedia of Textiles, Editors of American Fabrics Magazine, Doric Publishing Company, USA, 1972 (2nd edition).

Gioello, Debbie Ann, *Profiling Fabrics: Properties, Performance and Construction Techniques*, Fairchild Publications, New York, 1981.

Larsen, Jack Lenor and Weeks, Jeanne, *Fabrics for Interiors*, Van Nostrand Reinhold, Inc., New York, 1975.

Larsen, Jack Lenor with Alfred Bühler, Bronwen and Garrett Solyom, *The Dyer's Art*, Van Nostrand Reinhold, Inc., New York, 1976.

Larsen, Jack Lenor with Freudenheim, Betty, *Interlacing, The Elemental Fabric*, Kodansha International Ltd., USA, 1986.

Lubell, Cecil (ed.), *Textile Collections of the World*, Van Nostrand Reinhold Inc., New York, 1976.

Man-Made Fiber and Textile Dictionary, Celanese Corporation, New York, 1981.

Paine, Melanie, *Fabric Magic*, Pantheon Books, New York; Windward, UK, 1987.

Shoshkes, Lila, *Contract Carpeting*, Billboard Publications, Inc., New York, 1974.

Walch, Margaret and American Fabrics Magazine, *Color Source Book*, Charles Scribner's Sons, New York, 1971.

Wingate, Isobel B., *Fairchild's Dictionary of Textiles*, Fairchild Publications, New York, 1975 (6th edition).

Glossary

Abrasion resistance Durability of a fabric in the face of surface wear.

Abrasion tests Testing systems to compare a fabric's relative resistance to wear.

Analine dyed Usually pertains to dyeing top grain hides or skins with little or no further colorant or finish. Color is clearer, the hand is more sensuous than leathers colored with pigments, but fading and soiling often become more of a problem. Semi-analine dyed leathers (with some pigments applied after dyeing) are prudent choices for normal use.

Art Environment Usually of fabric or other maleable material, these dimensional, sometimes shrine-like spaces were (especially in the 1960s and 1970s) considered as "sculpture-to-be-in."

Axminster Machine-woven cut-pile carpet with jacquard patterning and, usually, many colors.

Backing A liquid or spray plastic back-coating for upholstery and wall fabrics to ensure dimensional stability or to resist slippage, raveling or fraying.

Basket weave A variation of plain weave in which two or more warp ends and an equal number of weft picks are woven as one.

Batik A resist print in which wax is drawn or blocked onto a fabric before dyeing.

Batting Layers or sheets of fiber used for lining quilts and upholstered walls.

Bird's-eye Traditional dobby-woven pattern of concentric diamonds.

Block printing General term for a hand-printing process using wood or linoleum blocks into which patterns have been cut.

Bouclé A novelty yarn that is looped to produce a pebbly surface.

Brocade (1) A weaving construction in which a supplementary warp and/or filling yarn is used to form a raised pattern. (2) A rich, jacquard-patterned cloth in brocade weave.

Calendering A standard finishing process in which a cloth is pressed heavily or repeatedly under a steel roller to produce a polished surface.

Canvas A dense cloth, originally cotton, in twill or plain weave.

Casement cloth A general term for sheer drapery fabric.

Chenille (1) A woven yarn or fabric woven of this yarn.

Chintz A glazed-cotton fabric, with or without a printed pattern, produced by applying resin and calendering.

Cloth count The number of warp ends plus the number of filling picks in an inch or centimeter of cloth.

Cloqué (French for blistered). Term for any fabric structure with raised or blistered surface. Usually these are double woven of two layers with different take-up or shrinkage.

Coir A coarse and extremely durable fiber obtained from the outer husk of coconuts.

Combing The process of laying long fibers parallel after carding and before spinning to produce a stronger, more lustrous yarn.

Crash A low-end cloth of slubby single-ply linen, cotton, or synthetic yarn.

Crêpe plissé Printed seersuckers created by applying an acid which elongates the fibers to create a dimpled surface.

Crocking The rubbing off of excess dyestuff from dry or wet fabric.

Cut pile A fabric or carpet in which the pile is cut rather than looped.

Damask A woven pattern based upon contrasting warp-face and weft-face areas.

Decoupé Primarily for transluscent window fibers; differentials in density are achieved by weaving long floats in some pattern areas then mechanically shearing them off after production.

Deposit printing Patterns created by screening a heavy, semi-liquid substance to achieve a surface in low relief.

Devoré The French term now used universally to describe burn-out or etched prints.

Dimensional stability The degree to which a fabric will retain its original shape or size.

Direction As related to fabrics, the relative tolerance of application. Those, like felt, that have no top or bottom and can be turned 90° are termed non-directional. Others, such as a botanical or pressed velvet, can only be used with one direction as 'up'.

Discharge printing A printing process in which the pattern is bleached out of already dyed goods; it may be replaced with another color.

Dobby An attachment for a multiple-harness loom that produces simple **dobby patterns**, such as bird's-eye.

Domestics Those washable furnishings fabrics for bed, bath, kitchen and table top.

Double cloth A compound cloth based on two sets each of warp and weft, held together at regular intervals by a warp or weft thread passing from one fabric to the other.

Double-faced fabric A reversible fabric, usually with one set of warp yarns and two sets of weft yarns, one on each face.

Double wefted Refers to those cloths woven with areas with one weft towards the face, one to the back. Reversing this order creates areas with another color and/or texture.

Dual-purpose cloths Those fabrics which are at least marginally suitable for both drapery and upholstery.

Duck A lightweight, plain-woven cotton canvas.

Duppioni A silk yarn reeled from two cocoons that have grown together, resulting in a slubby, interrupted texture.

Duvet A feather bed and its washable slipcase.

Embossing A decorative fabric finish produced by patterned rollers.

Embroidery A basic cloth embellished by ornamental needlework.

End-and-end cloth A plain-woven cloth, originally cotton, in which textural pattern is produced by alternating ends of dark and light yarns.

Fabric A term encompassing all kinds of cloth, and rugs, carpets, tapestries, mattings, canings, etc.

Face The side on which a fabric is finished.

Face weight As related to carpets, the weight (ounces/grams) of fiber in the pile per square yard/meter.

Faille A lightweight fabric, originally silk, with a pronounced transverse rib.

Felt (1) A fabric made from fibers not taken to yarn form but instead intermeshed by heat, moisture, and agitation. (2) A supported felt, formed over a meshlike armature to obtain additional strength. (3) A fabric made by shrinking and agitating woven or knit cloth to obtain superior density, resilience, and strength.

Fire codes As related to furnishings fabrics, those flame and smoke emission requirements for specific building types. Although these vary widely by end-use and locality, they become ever more stringent.

Flock prints Areas of the ground cloth are printed with glue then blown with short filaments to achieve the appearance of voided velvet.

Fold dyeing A form of tie-dyeing in which the cloth is first pleated, then wrapped very tightly to resist dye penetration.

Frieze A warp-pile fabric with uncut loops.

Fuzzing A gradual raising of fiber ends due to wear on the fabric surface, forming patches of matted fibers which retain soil and are unsightly in appearance.

Gauze An openly constructed, transparent cloth of any fiber.

Gimp A silk or metallic yarn spiral-wrapped closely around an inner core to cover it completely.

Glazing A general term for a polished finish on a cloth, often using waxes or resins and hot rollers.

Gobelin Tapestry made at the Gobelin works near Paris.

Grain The alignment of vertical and horizontal elements in a fabric, approaching a right-angle relationship.

Groundcloth or ground A cloth which is to be printed, embroidered, or otherwise embellished.

Half-tone screens Recently developed silk screens which subtly and smoothly shade from one color to another.

Hand Literally, the feel of the goods in the hand, a qualitative term used to describe the tactile properties of a fabric.

High-shrink Refers to yarns which, in fabric finishing, shrink so considerably as to distort the fabric surface.

Hopsacking A coarse, loose, plain- or basket-woven fabric of cotton or other yarns.

Hospitality A new term for the increasingly important hotel, restaurant, and club market.

Ikat   Patterns achieved by tying and dyeing yarns for warp or weft (or both) before weaving.

Jacquard   A pattern-controlling attachment for looms and knitting or lace machines.

Jacquard tapestry   Usually a heavy cotton upholstery jacquard woven with many sets of colored warps to achieve multicolored pattern.

Lace   An openly constructed, patterned cloth.

Laminated fabric   Fabric created by bonding two or more layers of material together.

Length-for-width   Describes wide window or wall fabrics turned 90° to be installed without seams.

Leno, or **marquisette**   A woven fabric construction in which two or more warp ends twist between insertions of weft.

Linen   A fiber extracted from the flax plant.

Matelasse   A jacquard-woven double cloth in which the pattern resembles a quilted surface.

Modacrylic   A generic term for a modified-acrylic fiber composed of copolymers of acrylonitrile and other materials such as vinyl chloride, which enable the fiber to be softened at low temperatures; does not meet all fire codes.

Mohair   The extremely long, silky fiber from the Angora goat.

Moiré   A popular wavy or watered pattern achieved by calendering two smooth, ribbed cloths one over the other. The ribs slip on each other to produce this effect. Moiré patterns are also simulated through jacquard damask patterning, embossing, or hanging two layers of sheer scrim.

Moresque   A yarn with plies of two or more colors used to produce a random pattern, especially in carpets and pile fabrics.

Muslin   A plain-woven, uncombed-cotton fabric, ranging from sheer to coarse in texture.

Nub   A random clot of short, dense fibers incorporated during spinning.

Obí   A broad sash, tied in a large flat bow at the back, worn as part of the Japanese national costume.

Open bed   See duvet.

Ottoman   A heavy horizontal-ribbed fabric, usually with a densely set warp of silk, acetate, or rayon, and a cotton or wool weft.

Paisley   A soft fine wool fabric traditionally woven or printed with a **paisley pattern** of small curving shapes with intricate detailing, usually in bright colors.

Panel fabrics   Cloth suitable for covering the acoustical wall panels of office systems furniture.

Panné   A mechanical finish for velvets and velours in which heat and pressure lay the pile on a steep diagonal, thus increasing pile cover and luster.

Paper yarn   A natural, bleached, or dyed yarn produced from twisted paper.

Passementerie   A fancy edging or trimming made of braid, cord, gimp, beading, or metallic thread.

Pattern   A structural or applied configuration that forms a unit of design.

Pattern repeat   A total design unit.

Pearlized lacquers   Real or imitation mother-of-pearl is first powdered, then mixed with synthetic printing lacquers to achieve a luminous glow.

Pick   An individual shot of weft yarn, often taken as a unit of the fineness of a fabric.

Pick-and-pick   The horizontal alternation of two yarns differing in texture or size but, usually color. The effect is similar to end-and-end.

Piece dyeing   The dyeing of cloth after production, as opposed to dyeing fibers or yarns before production.

Pigment   An insoluble powdered coloring agent carried in a liquid binder and printed or padded onto the surface of a cloth.

Pile   A velvety surface produced by an extra set of filling yarns that form raised loops, which may be cut and sheared or left uncut.

Pile weave   A fabric with cut or uncut loops above the surface of the ground cloth, such as terrycloth and velvet.

Pilling   Fuzzy balls caused by the rolling up of abraded surface fibers.

Plaid   A pattern of unevenly spaced repeated stripes crossing at right angles.

Plain weave   The simplest and most basic woven construction, in which one end interlaces alternately with one pick.

Plangi   The Maylay-Indonesian term for all forms of tie and dye fabric resists, including those done by folding, stitching, and knotting.

Polished cotton   A combed and carded fabric, usually of twill or satin construction, which is calendered to produce a high luster.

Quilting   The stitching together of two or more layers of fabric, generally separated by one or more layers of fiber batting.

Railroaded   Pertaining to those upholstery fabrics turned 90° in application.

Raveling   The fraying of yarns out of cut ends of cloth.

Raw silk   Silk that is not fully degummed; it is stiff, tacky, and naturally caramel in color.

Repp   A plain-woven fabric characterized by raised, rounded ribs running from selvage to selvage.

Resist, or **reserve**, **printing**   A general term for printing processes in which the motif or the ground is treated with a dye-resistant substance before dyeing the fabric.

Satin   A warp-faced woven construction in which the yarns are interlaced at widely spaced, regular or irregular intervals to form a smooth, compact, unbroken surface.

Schiffli embroidery   Machine-made embroidery in which the decorative yarns are held in place by a binder thread on the reverse side of the cloth.

Schiffli lace   A fabric produced by embroidering on a silk gauze, which is then burned away to create open areas.

Scouring   A finishing process in which warm or hot water is combined with soap or detergent to full the cloth and remove grease.

Screenprinting   A hand- or machine-printing process in which a pattern-making stencil or screen held in a frame or on a hollow roller, is positioned on the cloth, and colorant applied.

Scrim   A theatrical gauze of sheer, plain-woven linen or hemp.

Shading coefficient   The amount of heat-and light deflection achieved by a casement, an important factor in calculating a room's air-conditioning requirements.

Sheer   A very thin, transparent, or semiopaque fabric.

Shibori   The Japanese term for plangi resist fabrics.

Shirring   Fabric gathered into parallel folds or rows.

Shoji   A paper screen on a sliding wooden frame, used in Japanese houses as a room partition.

Side match   Particularly crucial for window and wall fabrics, this term refers to pattern alignment where panels join. Horizontal stripes are the most critical, so much so that some designers prefer slightly to mismatch all of them.

Sisal   A strong, coarse leaf fiber used primarily for cordage and carpeting.

Silk   A natural-protein fiber produced from the cocoon of wild or cultivated silkworms.

Slippage   A fabric fault caused by warp and weft yarns sliding on each other.

Slit film   A ribbonlike yarn cut from sheets of plastic or metallic films, in which metallic and other films are commonly available.

Slub   A heavy area in an unevenly spun yarn.

Staple   A fiber of relatively short length that is carded or spun, as opposed to such continuous filaments as reeled silk.

Stitch resists   These employ an open basting stitch which is pulled taut to produce a negative pattern when the cloth is dyed.

Striae   A series of parallel narrow bands of color, often darker than the ground color.

Sun rot   Deterioration caused by sun or light.

Swag   An ornamental festoon of drapery.

Systems furniture   Modular furniture systems for general offices which include communications equipment and task lighting, and the partitions between them.

Taffeta   (1) A crisp, plain-woven fabric in which the filling is heavier than the warp, producing a fine, lustrous rib. (2) Plain weave.

Tapestry   (1) A handweaving technique in which pattern is produced by interlocking discontinuous weft yarns. (2) A jacquard-woven warp brocade in which multicolored warp ends are carried on the back of the fabric.

Terrycloth   An uncut warp-pile fabric, plain- or jacquard-woven, of cotton, linen, or rayon.

Ticking   A heavy, strong, linen or cotton twill

with a colored warp stripe used in upholstering and as a covering for mattresses or pillows.

Transfer printing   A printing process in which a pattern is printed on waxed paper, then transferred to cloth under heat and pressure.

Trapunto   A decorative quilted design in high relief that is worked through two or more layers of cloth by outlining the design in a running stitch and padding it from the underside.

Tricot   A plain warp-knitted fabric with a close, inelastic vertical knit.

Tussah   A brownish silk from uncultivated oriental silkworms.

Tweed   A woolen fabric, usually of twill weave, with mixed color effects and a rough texture that derives from the yarn rather than the construction.

Twill   A basic weave in which the weft yarns pass over one or more and under two or more warp yarns in successive progression to create the appearance of diagonal lines.

Velvet   (1) A fabric with a short, soft, dense pile. (2) A woven fabric construction characterized by the insertion of an extra warp which is looped over wires and cut.

Voided   Pile fabrics with pattern areas of flat-woven ground cloth; usually velvets but may also be frieze or terrycloth.

Voile   A soft, sheer cloth plain-woven of fine crêpe-spun yarns.

Waffle weave   A piqué weave with a quadrangular pattern.

Warp   A series of yarns extending lengthwise on a loom and running parallel to the selvage.

Warp-faced   A cloth such as satin or faille in which the warp yarns dominate the face of the cloth.

Warp knit   A fabric produced on a knitting machine in which the yarns run in a lengthwise but zigzag direction.

Warp print   A pattern printed on the warp prior to weaving, which results in an indistinct image.

Weft, woof or **filling**   An element carried horizontally on a shuttle through the open shed of the vertical warp in a woven fabric.

Wilton   A Jacquard-woven patterned carpet. Pile may be cut, looped, or both.

Wrapped resists   These are bound with cord over folded or rolled cloth (for bound resists), or gathered and twisted areas of cloth (for true plangi) — both are types of plangi.

Wyzenbeek test   A test for abrasion resistance in upholstery fabrics.

Yarn   A continuous, often plied strand composed of fibers or filaments and used to form cloth.

Yoyo   The alternate sagging and shrinking of draped panels caused by humidity changes.

Shyam Ahuja
33/34 Dr. Annie Besant Road
PO Box 6594
Worli
Bombay
India

Almedahls AB
Almedahl-Kinna AB
Box 501
S-51101 Kinna
Sweden

ARTEK
Keskuskatu 3 PL 468
00101 Helsinki
Finland

ARTEK
Karlaplan 4
11460 Stockholm
Sweden

Art People
594 Broadway
New York
USA

ASSIA SpA
Tessuti Stampati e Tinti
Localita Batterello
20040 Briosco
Italy

Atelierdruck Kinderman KG
Theobaldgasse 16
Postfach 302
A-1061 Wien
Austria

Charles Barone
9505 Jefferson Blvd.
Culver City
CA 90232
USA

Baumann Weavers & Dyers, Ltd.
CH-4901 Langenthal
Switzerland

Ann Beetz
28 Rue de L'Arbe Benit
1050 Bruxelles
Belgium

BORAS Wafveri AB
PO Box 52
S-50102 Boras
Sweden

Boussac of France, Inc.
27 Rue du Mail
Paris 75002
France

Boussac of France, USA
979 Third Avenue
New York
NY 10022
USA

Brunschwig & Fils
979 Third Avenue
New York
NY 10022
USA

Brunschwig & Fils, UK
J. Pallu & Lake Furnishings, Ltd.
18 Newman Street
London W1P 4AR
England

Brunschwig & Fils, France
Les Tissues Casal
40, Rue des Saint-Peres
75007 Paris
France

Manuel Canovas, SA., UK
2 North Terrace
Brompton Road
London SW3 2BA
England

Manuel Canovas, SA., France
Place Furstenburg 75006
Paris
France

Manuel Canovas, SA, USA
979 Third Avenue
New York
NY 10022
USA

Carnegie Fabrics
110 North Centre Avenue
Rockville Center
NY 11570
USA

China Seas Inc.
979 Third Avenue
New York
USA

Christian Fischbacher Co. AG
Vadinstrasse 6
CH-9001 St. Gallen
Switzerland

Christian Fischbacher Co. AG
Threeways House
40/44 Clipstone Street
London W1P 8AL
England

Clarence House Fabrics, Ltd.
211 E. 58th Street
New York
NY 10011
USA

Coral of Chicago
2001 South Calmet Avenue
Chicago, ILL 60616
USA

Création Baumann
41–42 Berners Street
London W1P 3AA
England

De Angelis SpA
Via San Nicolo 3
20123 Milano
Italy

Design Tex Fabrics, Inc.
56-08 37th Avenue
Woodside
New York 11377
USA

Designers Guild
6 Relay Road
London W12 7SJ
England

Donghia Textiles, Inc.
315 E. 62 Street
New York City
USA

Teddy & Arthur Edelman, Ltd.
28 Hawleyville Road
PO Box 110
Hawleyville
Connecticut 06440
USA

Esteban Figuerola
Plaza Equilaz
10 entlo 2 08017
Barcelona
Spain

Etro
Via Spartaco, 3
20135 Milano
Italy

Facets Inc., USA
989 Avenue of the Americas
New York
USA

Finlayson
oy Finlayson AB
PO Box 407
33101 Tampere 10
Finland

Fujie Textile Co. Ltd.
No 4-17-12, Sendagaya
Shibuya-ku
Tokyo 151
Japan

Girmes AG
Johann-Girmes-Str.
Postfach 1120
4155 Grefrath 2
West Germany

Graber
A Division of Springs Industries, Inc.
Graber Plaza
Middleton
WI 53562-1069
USA

Gretchen Bellinger, Inc.
NYIDC
30–20 Thomson Avenue
Long Island City
NY 11101
USA

Helena Hernmarck
879 N. Salem Road
Ridgefield
Connecticut 06877
USA

Innovations In Wallcoverings, Inc.
22 West 21 Street
New York
NY 10010
USA

INTAIR/CPS Design
Stresemannallee 90
2000 Hamburg 54
West Germany

INTAIR/CPS Design U.S.A.
180 N.E. 39th Street
Miami
Florida
USA

International Linen Promotion Commission
200 Lexington Avenue
New York
NY 10016
USA

Jay Yang Designs Limited
41 Madison Avenue
New York
NY 10010
USA

Kinnasand AB
Box 256
S-51101 Kinna
Sweden

Boris Kroll Fabrics
979 Third Avenue
New York
NY 10022
USA

Kvadrat Bligtextiler AS
8400 Ebeltoft
Denmark

Kvadrat Ltd., UK
62 Princedale Rd
London W11 4NL
England

Jack Lenor Larsen, USA
232 E. 59th Street
New York
NY 10022
USA

Jack Lenor Larsen, Germany
Zimmersmühlenweg 14–18
6370 Oberursel
West Germany

Jack Lenor Larsen, France
Suzy Langlois SARL
266 Bd. Saint Germain
75007 Paris (14)
France

Jack Lenor Larsen, Great Britain
Clifton Textiles, Ltd
103 Cleveland Street
London W1P 5PL
England

Marc Raymond
16 West 23rd Street
New York
NY 10010
USA

Marks Pelle Vavare AB
Box 4039
S-5110 Kinna
Sweden

Marimekko
Puusepankatu 4
08810 Helsinki
Finland

Martex
A Division of Westpoint Pepperell
1221 Avenue of the Americas
New York
NY 10020
USA

Maya Romanoff Corp.
1730 W. Greenleaf Avenue
Chicago, ILL 60626
USA

Norelene
San Marco Campo 5. Maurzlo 2606
Venezia
Italy

NUNO Co., Ltd.
BI Axix Building
5-17-1
Roppongi
Minatoku
Tokyo
Japan

N.V. Albert Van Havere
Industriepark-Noord 13
B-2700 Sint-Niklaas
Belgium

Nya Nordiska
An den Ratswiesen
Postfach 1280
D-3138 Dannenberg
West Germany

O. J. Van Maele
Bedevaarlstraat, 21
B-8880 Tielt
Belgium

O. J. Van Maele, USA
48 Marlboro Industrial Park
Marlboro, New Jersey 07746
USA

Osbourne & Little PLC
49 Temperley Road
London SW12 8QE
England

Pausa AG
Postfach 1180
7406 Mossingen bei Tübingen
West Germany

Pontus USA
41 East 11 Street
New York City
NY 10003
USA

Carolyn Ray
578 Nepperhan Avenue
Yonkers
New York 10701
USA

Ben Rose
215 Park Avenue South
New York
USA

Ruckstuhl AG
PO Box 337
CH-4900 Langenthal
Switzerland

Rudd Textiles
1025 Thomas Jefferson Street
Washington, DC 20007
USA

Scalamandré
The Manzone Group
331 Park Avenue South
New York
NY 10010
USA

Sekers Fabrics Limited
15/19 Cavendish Place
London W1M 9DL
England

Silk Dynasty
Docey Lewis USA
PO Box 1048
Washington
CT 06703
USA

Monika Speyer
Wellenburgerstrasse 55
8900 Augsburg 22
West Germany

Steelcase
901 44 Street, S.E.
Grand Rapids
Michigan 49508
USA

Sunar Hauserman USA
730 Fifth Avenue
New York City
USA

Studio Tae
8 Josephine Avenue
London SW2 2LA
England

Jim Thompson Thai Silk Co., France
Suzy Langlois
266 Bd. Saint Germain
75007 Paris (14)
France

Jim Thompson Thai Silk Co., UK
Mary Fox Linton
249 Fulham Road
London SW3
England

Jim Thompson Thai Silk Co., USA
Rodolph, Inc. (Executive Office)
999 West Spain Street
PO Box 1249
Sonoma CA 95476-1249
USA

Timney/Fowler
388 Kings Road
London SW3 5UW
England

Unika Vaev
305 East 63 Street
New York
NY 10021
USA

Westinghouse Furniture Systems
4300 36th Street S.E.
Grand Rapids
Michigan 49508
USA

Zimmer & Rohde
Taunus Textildruck Zimmer KG
Oberurselerstrasse 83–85
6370 Oberursel
West Germany

Acknowledgements

The publishers and the author would like to thank all the fabric designers and manufacturers who submitted work for inclusion in this book, and the following photographers for use of their material: Jaime Ardiles-Arce (*170, 211*); David Arky (*130*); Chris Cassidy (*6–7*); Fabric Workshop (*24–5*); Grauel and Uphoff (*154*); Lennart (*92 left*); Mauss (*188–9*); Norman McGrath (*186*); Peter Olsen (*40–41, 42, 50–51, 55, 57 left, 59, 66–7, 73, 74, 78, 88 above and below, 95, 104 center and right, 122 center, 124, 126 center and below, 135 left and above right, 138–9, 140 above, 143, 149, 151, 152–3, 162 below, 163 above, 164 below left*); Olson, Sweden (*85 above and below*); Richter and Fink (*187*); Walter Smalling Jr. (*223*); Ezra Stoller (*213*); Studio Henrik Schutt KY, Helsinki (*184*).

Index